THE SECRET LIFE
OF THE
VERY OLD

A VIEW FROM THE SUMMIT

Gemma d'Auria and Antonia Burgato

Zanon Indie Press
Westlake Village, California

Copyright © 2020 Antonia Burgato
ISBN: 978-1-7348213-0-7
All rights reserved. No part of this publication may be reproduced, stored in a retrieval system, or transmitted in any form or by any means, electronic, mechanical, recording or otherwise, without the written permission of the author.
Published by BeeZee Press, Westlake Village, CA,
For information contact the author at www.antoniaburgato.com

In Memory of Gemma
d'Auria and her son Robert
Houston, my late husband,
who died just two years after
his mother.

Contents

NOTES FROM THE AUTHORS	1
GROWING NEW	7
THE GRADUATING CLASS	13
THE TRANQUIL MEADOW	20
ALLVIEW TERRACE	25
CONCERNING NEW FREEDOMS	30
ON THE TORTOISE PORCH	37
UNDERGROUND RIVERS	42
WEAVING A NEW GARMENT	47
A FAMILIAR PLACE	50
ROUNDED STONES	57
LINK BY LINK	62
BEYOND THE WITHERED LEAF	68
WITH ONE WORD	74
ENOUGH IS ENOUGH	78
EXCHANGE FOR THE BETTER	86
NOT ABOUT LONELINESS	91
DRAWING FROM LIFE'S SAVING ACCOUNT	95
THE BEQUEST OF LOVE	100
SORTING FOR TOMORROW	107
THE CITADEL WITHIN	111
THE GRADUATES	118

NOTES FROM THE AUTHORS

From Antonia Burgato

I met Gemma d'Auria when she was in her eighties, and I less than half her age. She came from an old Philadelphia society, without a thought about finances, and I was an immigrant struggling to make ends meet. We could not have been more different from each other. We came from different worlds in social standing, education, economic status, and age. There was little to nothing that we had in common. Yet, we could sit side by side for hours then retire fully satisfied from a feast of silent and verbal communication.

What magic there was in our time together could, perhaps, best be understood by comparing it to the symbiotic relationships in the animal and plant life. The clownfish and anemone, for example, with nothing in common beyond their water world, benefit from each other's company by providing food by the former and shelter from predators by the latter. Plants, too, have their symbiotic relationships with one another other. The fungi and the algae coexist to produce lichen. Rosemary planted near sage, cabbage, and carrots will keep away flies, and marigolds with their scent help tomatoes and roses grow. So it could be seen that the relationship between Gemma and me was symbiotic—the elder with a desire to share her life's learning with the neophyte eager to learn from her—a teacher-pupil relationship, if you will.

She lived on a hill overlooking Hollywood and seldom went out. Everything she needed was at home, she said. Her garden was an overgrown hodgepodge of twisted branches bending to the ground, and that was the way she liked it. In her house, the walls were lined with bookshelves full of disorderly books and knickknacks that, to her clear logic, were in perfect order, which she proved by knowing exactly where to find any item. She was a poet, a classical dancer (she had danced at the Ziegfeld Follies), a sculptor, and a naturalist who studied the nature around her.

After she died, her son gave me her typewritten book, The Secret Life of the Very Old, some two hundred pages, of what she had learned about life and aging as the path to a peaceful end to existence on earth.

We are all pilgrims in this life, traveling to our special place of significance, wherein dwells the source of the fountain of our Being. What or where this place is depends on the road we take. The path and each turn we make are teachable units in the school of life. There are many twists and turns to make before reaching the final lesson.

The young and the very old are at opposite points in the road, and they have different goals, and this difference is the stuff of misunderstanding that often separates them. The young look forward to a time when they have mastered their responsibilities and have earned the freedom to enjoy an unencumbered life. The very old celebrate the gifts of successful aging: the wisdom and mastery that Dr. Gen. D. Cohen, author of *The Mature*

Mind: The Positive Power of the Aging Brain, defines as the human experience that requires decades of learning. They have mastered the lightness of Being and accepted leaving the physical world for one unencumbered by the hullabaloo of mortal life.

I submitted the book to a couple of publishers who had good things to say but found it too poetic and of limited value to attract a broad readership. I disagreed. While her writing was abstract and bursting with florid adjectives, the content was compelling. I endeavored to rewrite the book with an active voice, removing poetic attributes but maintaining her poised voice.

The *Secret Life of the Very Old* is even more relevant today, thirty-five years after Gemma's death, with more couples delaying children and parents living longer. The squeeze between raising a family and caring for parents for a prolonged period gives rise to frustration, impatience, and irritability. The aged parent feels this. This book presents a view from the summit of Gemma d'Auria's life when a map of paths taken and missed is visible for examination.

From Gemma d'Auria

Today the world faces a widening gap in understanding between children and parents, people and government, minority groups, and the overpowering majority. However, a wider gap separates the young, active men and women from the very old, who live in the serene plateau that rises at the far side of life. And yet the young—and by the young, I mean those still oriented to the business of living in this world—often find themselves responsible for the comfort and care of the old who live in an entirely different state of awareness.

The immediate business of the young centers around events that make up the pattern of life, which repeats itself as surely as the recurring seasons. The young are occupied with education, career, family, children, and social engagements—the civil and ethical responsibilities incorporated into the daily actions that affect people and their environment. The young are forever in motion, and, yet, do not go anywhere, for they are earthbound.

The very old are like people about to embark on a journey, waiting at an airport for the plane's departure. They are not concerned with the temporary surroundings nor the meaningless bustle around them but with lessening their baggage in preparation for the journey to their final destination.

The preparation for this time, says Dr. J. G. Jung, begins as soon as we have reached middle life. It is not an ending, but a goal and a beginning and is an integral part of life. The line that depicts the life of the body and brain moves downward to the childlike struggle for independence. But the physical body becomes arrested from the self by the time we reach old age. Dr. Jung refers to this separation as "the detachment of the consciousness from the object."

Few people experience the in-between period of detachment and indifference to their surroundings until just before they are ready to leave. But most of the very old are fortunate to do so because the limited mental functions no longer interfere with correcting, negating, and attempting to set conditioned ideas against the laws of life. Thus, unhampered, the self can be prepared for the transition to whatever awaits the freed consciousness.

I pen these pages to close the gap and to offer a glimpse of the purpose and beauty of age, for age is the highest point of the ascending line on the graph of life. With these pages, I hope to open the curtain, however slightly, to reveal the beauty of aging.

I walked the path up on the hill
Careful to sidestep the canvas at my feet
Of flaming reds and orange and purple plains
The poppies and the lupines and the red maids
Danced beneath the sun in gentle warming
breeze
And
The sun was high and the field in full view
I walked the fields of desert bloom

Found among Gemma d'Auria's writings. No author attribution is given. I assume it to be hers.

GROWING NEW

We are the very old. We are a mystery. However, to you, who attend to our needs during our dependent years, we are mostly a problem. How could you feel otherwise? You see us as what we seem—shrunken, wrinkled, and broken—and judge us by the same standards as when we were young—a time when we had set a course to achieve a goal as much as you do now. We do not set goals anymore; at least none that would fit in the spiritual world we are about to enter. From the summit of our years, we have a view of the life we have lived stretched before us like a map, charting every road we have taken to where it has led us. Turning points in our lives stand out in sharp images, and we learn the full implication of decisions that have set things on the inevitable course toward our final path. We have studied our charted course from infancy to maturity to seniority and learned from it with twenty-twenty hindsight.

It is problematic enough for human beings to understand each other, even when they share the same goals, and their age is the same. However, a rift occurs in understanding us, who live in a different dimension of existence—although it should not. Complimentary words defining the very old are few: sage, wise, and mature, come to mind—while derogatory terms defining the very old abound: over-the-hill, out-to-pasture, retired, codger, senile, old goat, and crone are a few from a long list. It would help to reexamine the words used to define the aged— words that once were accurate descriptions but now create a false image. Because we think with words and respond to pictures, the words used to describe us should echo what we are.

"Old" is a word covered with a false patina. When you use the word "old," no doubt you think of a person diminished to uselessness. Yet, "old" once meant to grow up, to achieve. As it came chiseled from the Icelandic, it meant nourished, brought up, or grown up. Later, this meaning evolved with the Latin *altus*, high, to portray those men and women who had been nourished and brought up to a high state of development. Then there is "mature," which means almost the same as "old." It stems from the Latin *matura*, meaning ripeness, or completeness of growth, as in mature fruit. "Elderly" is another form of "elder" and once referred to one who, having reached an esteemed age, occupied the office of judge or ruler. Today the word "elderly" is used in some churches. The Elders are an order of priesthood. Even "senile" has a fine, proud beginning. We refer to the "Senate," once a council of the "senile," who were men old enough to be wise rulers. Today these words project an image of forced retirement, lost powers, and final decay. With their present meanings, these words do not apply to us.

We, who have had the opportunity to gain wisdom from our many years on earth, do not think of ourselves as old. "Old" is like the word "there." We are never there. We can only be here, and the time we occupy is always now—never the future. The future, like age, never comes. To a thirty-year-old man, sixty seems old. When he arrives at sixty, ninety seems old, and so on, moving the number of years toward some mathematical infinity. For us, old age, like the horizon, always lies ahead—that vague, blue vanishing point where the earth and the heavens meet.

This view of ours must seem strange to you. Doubtless, you picture us silhouetted against the increasing darkness of night, standing on some far ridge—the jumping-off place of the world. But we hope that with a little sympathetic imagination, you may identify with us and ascend to our place and view the vast country that stretches below us.

Communication between us may start by sharing this view, for you need assurance that our time in life, which one day will be yours, is worthy and purposeful. We would be grateful for your understanding, your respect, and your love.

So, let us emphasize that we are not growing old—no one ever grows old. The word "grow" comes from *growan*, the Anglo-Saxon, and means to spring up and mature, to thrive, to increase in any way, to become larger, stronger. Yet, when you say "growing old," you think of a process of becoming less. We accept that we are growing old but not that we are growing less. We grow differently. We grow new. All life grows toward perfection and fulfillment, and it will continue until the growth is complete. It is no different from a budding blossom on a tree in the spring, which changes to a green leaf in the summer and a golden leaf in the fall until it withers away to nourish the ground that gave it life, and then grows new again.

We, too, grow new.

In a poem by Robert Browning, we read that "The best is yet to be, the last of life, for which the first was made." We know the truth of this assertion because we experience this truth now. Life is an ever-ascending line shaped like a pyramid that rises to a peak at the center and then falls. If you think about the design of this ascending graph, warm the truth of it against your heart as peasant women used to warm eggs for hatching. It may break through the brittle shell of words and become a living certainty for you as it has for us. Recognizing this truth could bring comfort on dark days when a vision of our latter years looms large and frightening

The summit of this earth phase of life is the flowering of all the earlier years—a harvest of wisdom. The prime of life is a physical prime only. It is the prime of our strength, of our keenness of sight, of our sharpness of hearing, of memory. It is the peak of our ability to work in the home, the office, the community. In pioneer countries like the United States, the pattern of our settlers is still valued. The strength to fight, build, and clear fields for planting an Appalachian spring continues to be admired even after modern inventions have made them obsolete.

You should not measure us by these standards, nor do we intend to measure ourselves by any such unsuitable gauge. What could have been the worth of an Albert Einstein if society had valued him according to his ability to dig a ditch? Our worth lies in another field and has nothing to do with how well we can remember, or of what practical use we can be to anyone. You understand our attempts to adjust to a life of diminishing returns. You see us striving to develop new interests to replace those we once had, exchanging competition in business for competition in shuffleboard, the care of children, or home for the care of begonias or African violets.

You may look at this as "less life," and for a while, we also see it this way. This period is like the neutral position between gears on a stick shift. Before pushing forward into high gear comes an in-between place where the car, if it moves at all, does so on its old momentum with no help from the engine. This out-of-gear time is difficult. We have passed through this time and now move forward safely in high gear on the new road before us.

We often talk of events that happened years ago in another place, as though they are happening here and now. There-and-now is our only reality. Sometimes we speak in a language that is gibberish to you but has meaning for us. You see a superfluous part of us—the shedding husk. Yet all the while, in the corn of our secret selves, stirs the next spring's growth, and we wait to feel the first pulse of our new life. Our eyes no longer focus on the world. They gaze inward, toward a dawn that brightens over the shadowy past. We grow to be like little children again— wise children ready for a new beginning.

There is a custom among many American Indian people of folding the ancient ones into the posture of the yet-to-be-born when they return them to the womb of the Earth Mother, there to sleep their way into the next life. This return to earth is the curving gesture of all tired things. Our bodies are worn things, but we are not our old bodies—we are growing new.

THE GRADUATING CLASS

We, who are growing new, are members of the graduating class of life. We have completed our work in all the lower grades. Life's lessons do not begin at some stated hour in the morning, do not end at any specified time, and do not have recess and weekends off. The classes are in session every moment of the day and night, for even in our dreams we learn. The lesson ends when we face a challenging situation—a death in the family, the loss of a job, an unexpected expense, a fight with our spouse. This is the time for our test. We do not know that it is an examination. Whatever the case, how we answer the challenge is our test paper.

The first thought should be to look at the situation and ask whether this is something under our control. If not, as difficult as it might be, we must let it go and look for courage and peace within our inner selves. We turn inward through meditation or practice yoga. When we find inner peace, our mind becomes calm, and we accept the loss and move on to the next lesson. If the situation is something within our control, we rely on the support and compassion of friends or seek professional help. Sometimes, a solution is evident, and we take action. At other times, we take small steps toward a conclusion, or settle for a compromise. A vision for the future is always the goal, and how one sees it varies from person to person.

Sometimes we employ a strategy that combines a peaceful time for inner thought followed by action. I recall a distant friend who lived in Louisiana during the flood of 1973. The overflow of the Mississippi River had destroyed his house, and his father died a week later from sudden heart failure. Both events were out of his control. There was nothing he could do about the past. He had to let it go. What he could control was how to move forward. "The past is gone," he said. "I must look to the future and act on the things I can control." He was thinking of his wife and three children. His workplace was temporarily closed due to damage, but he could return to it soon. He had a minimal traditional education, worked as a freighter in the shipping industry, and possessed an inspiring understanding of the lessons from life.

The grief of two losses within a short time subjected him to emotions ranging from shock to anger to guilt and profound sadness. To deal with it, he relied on the support of friends and the financial help from FEMA for the situation that he could control—the long term vision to rebuild a home for the future with his family. The house was a material loss that could be replaced. However, the loss of the parent could not be replaced. For that, he turned to meditation and prayer. Although the memory of his father remained with him, the pain of grief would eventually abate.

We must answer to all the challenges presented to us. No matter how cleverly we may try to evade the questions that life-the-teacher presents to us, sooner or later, we must answer them. We must choose between at least two possibilities. Limited though we are and conditioned by what seems desirable to us, we have enough free will to choose between this and that. Whatever we finally decide upon, that becomes the answer in our test.

Sometimes we employ a strategy that combines a peaceful time for inner thought followed by action. In the graduating class, some students have done very well. Others have received low grades or have not completed their work. But even they will graduate when their time comes. Some of us are thankful that we are in the graduating class at all. To be here is an achievement because the lessons have never been easy. Our place of honor in the graduating class is a chair by the window, or a bed, or a wheelchair. We are not merely sitting there marking time until our release—killing time, as it were.

Nothing could be further from the truth. Time is more precious to us now than ever, and we cherish every moment, for we are still students, and these days are a final recapitulation. We work on that examination, presented at the end of a course of study, called "comprehensive" since it covers all that we have learned. Our final grade depends on our answers. The questions that confront us now are fundamental. What do you value most in your life? Or, How do you explain consciousness? The questions arise from the center of our Being, and we must answer them from there, without words. There is no one correct answer. Each person has a different Being, and the response varies according to his culture and ideology. Life-the-teacher has taught us the answers to these questions, which dwell deep inside our still center.

From the view of our summit, we see a retrospective slideshow of every lesson from the school of life. Senseless pain is tough to bear, but we accept a corrective operation with courage, knowing that it helps our healing. Grief and hardship break us into a very natural rebellion until we see that all misfortune is part of a vast system of teaching. The lessons we receive are what we need at the time of our growth. We experience happiness and unhappiness and discover what brought about happiness and what caused the lack of it. We have a time for tranquility and a time for suffering.

Do you recall how you taught your small children not to place their hands on a hot air vent?

"No," you said.

Then, as the spoken word went unheeded, you tapped the reaching hand. Then again you tapped, harder. If this did not work, you stood by, alert and watchful, and allowed the small fingers to come close to the hot surface, only close enough to learn about consequences, sparing the ignorant mind all that it could spare and still be forewarned.

As we review our valuable experiences, we see this method of teaching at work. We recall that often a warning is not enough, that we must go all the way to pain, to grief, before we learn what not to touch. There is a positive way of teaching us also.

From our high place, we see the plan laid out like a map. We see around every corner. We understand how we chased one small happiness to another, how we followed the lollipop trail of rewards from sweet to sweet, from smaller to greater satisfaction until we understood the relationship between what we did and how we felt afterward. We see the law of cause and effect as it works out in our life. However, this is often difficult to detect. We are inclined to look for an immediate manifestation while the outcome might be long delayed and hidden. From our lofty perch, we see that one always reaps in the end what one has sown in the beginning.

The good seeds that we drop in the darkness of our secret thoughts bloom in the light when we most appreciate beauty and light. But they are not visible to the eye that looks for wealth, or glamour, or authority. If the flowering shows at all, it is covered by radiance. Many of the so-called primitive people of the world, like some of the American Indians, have this radiance. We recognize it from the light they shine through their love of nature. This light is love—the intuitive connection with men, earth, sea, and sky. Love is the only thing that we, in the graduating class, long for. We crave for the nourishment of our inner being more than that of our bodies. We often leave the soup in the bowl to grow cold and the mashed potatoes untouched. This food we can do without. But how hard it is to do without love! How hungry we are for love!

Respect, too, we would like to have. Our ways are not your ways—not any longer. Ours are the ways of those about to graduate from this school of life. It is difficult to understand us as it is difficult for a high school student to understand the concerns of a college senior. Higher mathematics, the advanced sciences, the fine arts are a mystery to those who are still learning arithmetic, memorizing the names of the planets, or studying the lives of famous painters. Still, the young have a natural respect for the older.

There is a vibrant, fully intentional life within us, just beyond our powers of communication. The thought of our graduation warms us with anticipation. We recall the expectation that comes at a concert when the conductor lifts his baton, and the orchestra awaits his signal. We now feel the same thrill that passes through an audience in the hush just before the curtain rises. You have all known a nameless thrill at times. You might have had a foretaste of something you had not dreamed of, seen a vision that would make it possible for you to welcome the years to come, for we are happy.

Do you remember how, as a child, you awoke one beautiful morning with a rush of excitement ringing like bells in your heart? At first, your still-sleeping memory could not name the cause of such happiness. All you knew was that you had this feeling, this bright joy. Later you recalled that this was Christmas Day or your birthday or that you were going fishing. But at first, there had been only the nameless anticipation. That is the way knowledge comes to us now—with a catch of the breath, with a leap of the heart.

At first, we do not identify this anticipation with the opportunity ahead. But by holding our attention upon this fleeting glimpse, the certainty opens before us. We share this knowledge with you so that in understanding us, you might come to understand your own life better when you arrive at that place where we are now. In this way, you can look forward to the day when you, too, will be in the highest class and will walk the long aisle of honor to where the president of all colleges waits to bestow upon you a diploma for a task well done, a purpose accomplished *cum laude*.

THE TRANQUIL MEADOW

It is night. The city is as quiet as a city can be. There is only the muted hum of distant traffic as it flows through the arteries of the freeways.

I lie awake in the house on the hill thinking of you who, through love or duty, care for us at our time of graduation. It worries you that we lie awake so much. You wonder if you should give us a sleeping pill or a glass of hot milk. You think sleeplessness is as distressing to us as it is to you. But we seldom expect nights of uninterrupted slumber. Scattered wakefulness interrupts our sleep, and catnap pauses fracture our wakeful days.

We have gone beyond extremes in our living, emotions, reactions, and opinions. We have left behind the jagged peaks and deep ravines of our up-and-down younger days, and we have arrived at a tranquil meadow. All our lives, we have had to face responsibilities. We have had to confront oncoming events and make difficult decisions. Responsibilities, activities, decisions—each contributed to our learning process necessary at the time. We could avoid the challenge without having the problematic business repeat itself. But now we have reached a quiet place. You do not expect us to solve tricky business anymore.

Even time is different for us. There is no clock watching. We mislay our wristwatch and never miss it! There is no need to turn the leaves of the calendar nor to write the exact hour of appointments. The world has ceased to depend on our punctuality. Our time has left the bondage of those nest-tight-little containers such as minutes, days, and years and has begun to diffuse like a mist over the vast stretch of eternity. At present, we foretaste what this timelessness will be. We are learning how to move in it. Is it any wonder that we forget what day it is, or what month? Even the boundary and sequence of the years are no longer clear. So, when you visit us, we may not be able to recall your name or even your relationship to us, or when you last dropped by. But never doubt that the warm comfort of your love surrounds us for a long while. Your visit has not been a waste of time.

We tire quickly—long before the visiting hours are over. Our span of attention appears short. But that is because you break our quiet expanse of near timelessness into many shattered pieces. Your voices are tense with a sense of fleeting minutes—minutes that you give to us when you have so much else to do. You do not seem able to share our tranquil silence without fidgeting in a sort of frustration. You feel you are not getting through to us, that we are not aware of your presence. You make animated attempts to attract our attention on your terms and in your time, which is your present.

How pleasant it would be if you could meet us in our time and show interest when we tell of some event that occurred thirty years ago, according to the legend on your calendar, but which has just happened now in the fusion of past and present that we experience. These little vignettes of people or events, which are ancient history to you, rise into focus, and we like to talk about them. And why should they be of less interest to you because they happened half a century ago rather than two days? Often, when we refer to anything not in the immediate present, we observe a glazed look coming into your eyes. The kind of look that says, poor mother, or poor uncle Bill, is becoming confused.

The times when we talk in what you consider a rambling manner will become less and less frequent until we will scarcely speak at all. Then it would please us if you could sit quietly beside us and hold our hands or stroke our foreheads—just giving and receiving the wordless, timeless gift of love. It is in terms of this spirit of love that we measure your visit and your ministrations. The flowers that you bring to us wither in the sterile, unloving atmosphere of a hospital. The care and comfort you give us from a sense of duty or to avoid guilt after we have gone is already a withered thing. But the love that may go with the slightest gesture, the smallest offering, the gentlest silence, will remain a warm, close presence in a world that grows ever more distant. And this love is a treasure we take with us.

No place, condition, or relationship is right unless we make it so. Do you remember how it was when you needed a vacation to "get away from it all"? Your nerves were taut with frustrations. Small annoyances crept into your dreams, and your sleep was a sea of anxieties. Somewhere out there, you thought, there surely is a quiet, warm place on the gold and blue stretches of the desert or in the mountains where you could find peace. Perhaps you found such a place and planned to go there. You vowed you would leave all your vexing problems at the office or home. But when vacation became a reality, and you were in the peaceful beauty of the desert or the mountains, was it really like this? Few holidays are what one hopes for because of all the troubles and tensions associated with them. Just moving from one place to another is of little help. The only right place for a perfect vacation is within one's self. We have learned this truth. We have created our vacation place over the years within the center of our being. We have earned every foot of our tranquil meadow because we have made it, and now we have the right to dwell in it.

If you really see us when you look at us, you will be aware that we experience a deep and gentle peace without being troubled by any sense of selfishness. We know this tranquil place is ours. Soon enough, we will be called away to another classroom to continue our learning toward perfection. But now, when we need to leave this world, we know where to go and how to get there. Not for anything would we return to that persistent inner drive, that incessant pushing, that sense of failure and guilt if we do not get somewhere.

Does our tranquil meadow seem as attractive to you as it does to us? In our new state, peaceful vistas open before us. When the family has retired, after the visitors have left, and we are through with supper, we retreat to this new, timeless state, this tranquil meadow—our reward for a trying life.

We look forward to our meditations in the quiet of the night, to give ourselves over to Existence as we listen to the music of the dark with its obligato of crickets, the sound of cars on the distant freeway, the bark of a neighbor's dog. Then we can rest upon the infinite ocean of peace as a seabird rests upon the dark waters. We can feel the rise and fall of our breath that is like the rise and fall of the sea of all-loving Existence, which restores us forever.

ALLVIEW TERRACE

We of the graduating class have reached the top of the mountain with a full view of the commotion below. That plateau, where my house is, circles a knoll. The knoll is the highest ground anywhere here. To the east, the land slopes down to Bronson Canyon. Beachwood Canyon, with its palm trees and acacias, lies below to the west, and a wide expanse of the city spreads to the south. Beyond the city lies the vast Pacific Ocean.

On a clear afternoon, when the sun is low, a narrow ribbon of gleaming light marks the line of the watery horizon. Legend has it that on days of extraordinary clearness, you can see the island of Santa Catalina far across the channel.

From the hilltop, I see all the activity below, all that living; I see it not with indifference but with detachment. Now, instead of being involved, I can stand to one side and learn from it. The whole city, which seemed huge when I was lost among its poorly marked streets, now appears small enough to cover with a glance. I can read it like a familiar book that lies open before me with its beginning, its heightening suspense of middle, and falling resolution. It is there to learn—the display of accomplishments and failings visible to all who have lived through every test of life and taken the final exam. We read the expanse of experience behind us the way we see the view stretching below.

To live on a hill, in a physical sense, is not essential. I have used this description of my home as an analogy only. Now that we understand that every object around us, every event, every relationship can reveal some law, some truth, we find ourselves making analogies to discover this law—the one assignment given to the post-graduate class.

Several people live on the hill where I do. But after the novelty of the view wore off and habit had dulled their sight, some have stopped looking. The actual hill is not essential—pleasant, but not necessary. Everyone in the senior class lives on a high hill with their retrospective of life stretching below, like a city view.

In a symbolic sense, there are still higher elevations for us to reach, just as there are greater heights for the dwellers on the plateau where I live. For to the north of Allview Terrace, the Santa Monica Mountains rise as a guide for the dweller on the hill as the North star does for the sailor at sea.

I am always aware of these mountains to the north, watching for the changing light to play variations of color on their gaunt and rugged peaks—violet and rose for dawn, a milky pink for the sundown, indigo-purple for the night.

I have never climbed those mountains, although they appear to be only a few miles away, but have always known that one day I would pack a lunch and start. But not today. I have not begun to exhaust the beauty and meaning available to me from the vantage point of the plateau.

The mountains are not for us yet, with our tired hearts and our weary legs. The mountains are an assuring promise that that something lies ahead, that there is something still more beautiful to achieve, that our hilltop is not the ultimate height.

You, who live as a flatlander, are unable to see around the corners of your flat streets, unable to know how two roads meet beyond your horizon. Some people have added the dimension of height to those of length and breadth as a place to live. That is where we live. We live high.

Many ambiguous signposts mark the road we climbed to this place. Some would have redirected us to where we started. We were wise to avoid these wrong turns and the side roads, which led nowhere.

We knew enough to bypass the temptation of camping, where a signpost assured us we were going in the right direction. We learned that "This is the way" did not mean "This is the destination." Many travelers bog down this way, mistaking a method for an accomplishment, a ritual for an illumination.

As you see us sitting in our favorite chair, a faint smile on our lips, you may wonder at our idleness. We are busy remembering all the right roads we have taken, all the signposts which we recognized for what they are, all the cul-de-sacs that did not tempt us.

I remember the time I visited an amusement park when I was a child. One of the chief attractions was the Maze of Mirrors. I entered between confusing reflections until I lost all sense of direction. That was great fun until I became lost among reflections of reflections, and desired parental arms that seemed very far.

In our immature days, we lived under similar conditions. You live this way now—among images that are not what they appear and on roads that lead nowhere. We, too, made many mistakes, but our right decisions outweighed the wrong. We learned the signs of the right path, the one that led us to happiness. We learned how to distinguish between what was real and what reflected the real—an imitation.

But to return to the Maze of Mirrors. As I recall, there was always a "man on top." He sat high above the maze to look down into all the curving aisles and direct the befuddled player. This man on top had the same view of the maze that we now have of the whole of our life. We, too, can see the overall design. We can see what roads promised to go on forever but stopped at a woodpile and what streets ended or curved around a corner. The beginning and the destination are visible to us.

We know where the road of love makes the journey only halfway. And we can trace the lengthy roundabout way of self-delusion. We have learned as much from taking the wrong roads as well as the right ones. It would help if a notice here and there, announced that this is not a through street. But people seldom learn from the mistakes of others because no two people react in the same way, and no two situations are alike. You must investigate for yourself how a man can make a fool of himself.

We look at you long and silently and wish to warn you of the rough and disastrous goings that lie on the path you have chosen. But that is not possible.

As we ascended to this high place and, as our view extended to include an ever-increasing expanse of life, we learned that we could not direct any life but our own. By one path or another, and in good time, you, too, will have reached a hilltop view.

CONCERNING NEW FREEDOMS

We have arrived at the time of life when we can claim freedom from all responsibility.

You, who still live during your active years, do not see the burden of the responsibility you carry around all day and which lies like an oppressive weight upon your sleep. Not only do you feel the need to do something for your immediate family, but you may also wish to better the condition of the community, the nation, and the people everywhere. Besides, you may be the person who believes that all this bettering depends on your efforts.

Can you move from under this weight for a moment and imagine how it would be if you were like us from whom nothing is asked and very little expected except to cause the least trouble to anyone? Would you consider the lack of responsibility a loss, a demotion?

It is not. To be free from responsibility is one of the most gracious privileges given to us; it is far from a demotion. Rather, it is a promotion, a reward that we, who have lived long, claim.

We need not feel the bite of conscience for not hurrying here and there to attend to the many things that your world calls important. We have moved up to that peaceful state where we have the right not to feel guilty about neglecting a need we are not aware of, be it in a personal relationship or an impersonal. Birthdays and anniversaries have little meaning to us. When we find it impossible to remember who is running for what office, it is because time has freed us from any duty to be civic-minded or politically conscious.

Another bondage from which we have been freed is memory. The lack of it would seem to you a hardship, but you consider this lack in us a sign that we are "falling to pieces" or are in a state of senility. A brain stored with memories is like an attic piled to the rafters with the accumulations of a lifetime regardless of value or lack of it.

In the past, such attics were a familiar sight, with their old furniture, their ancient trunks, with books that no one would read again. The owners once expected to throw out the unwanted junk. But they seldom got around to it unless they had to move.

The flowers that you bring to us wither in the sterile, unloving atmosphere of a hospital. The care and comfort you give us from a sense of duty or to avoid guilt after we have gone is already a withered thing. But the love that goes with a caress, the tender hand-holding, the gentlest silence, will remain a warm, close presence in a world that grows ever more distant. And this love is a treasure we take with us. During most of our lives, we found it necessary to sustain a state of alertness. Lack of vigilance brought a swift penalty—a loss of job, a harmful accident, or even cause or become a victim of a disaster. We no longer need to be ready for an emergency. We need not always be on our toes in business encounters or in bargaining of any kind.

And there is the freedom from a game we used to play—the game of being a character. Only yesterday, we tossed it on the throw away pile. Once, it was a useful game. As a character, we were sought after, and we sometimes demeaned ourselves to be wanted for whatever reason. We became conversation pieces. Relatives liked to talk about us, joshing our idiosyncrasies. The character that we allowed ourselves to become was full of quick, tart replies, of cane-wagging, no-young-scalawag-is-going-to-tell-me sort of attitudes. Friends visited us as they would visit a monkey in a zoo and afterward would keep the family entertained for hours repeating our snappy remarks. "Aunt Hazel is as sharp as a whip, and she must be ninety if a day!" Or "Old man Higgins doesn't let any grass grow under his feet. They don't come like that anymore."

To gain attention, any attention, many of us sacrificed our dignity and that of others in our graduating class. We played our amusing parts to buy a little acceptance, to receive a few more visits, and we smiled. But now the tired muscles can rest. We smile when we feel like it. But always, our expression is the natural result of our emotions.

I should have learned about the sincerity of expression years ago, for when I was seven years old, I had my first encounter with a person who did not think it necessary to stretch his lips in greeting. The man came to call on the family. He was sitting on the couch, very relaxed, and my first impression was of his very great age. When I was introduced to him, I extended my hand and smiled, as I had learned to do. The man accepted not only the limp fingers but the whole small hand, surrounding it with a warm, firm clasp, but he made no expected remark. And he did not smile.

The unusual greeting confused and embarrassed me, not only for myself but for him because he had not done what was polite. As I thought over the incident, the uppermost impression was of the warm friendliness shown in his eyes. And I admired his courage in daring not to conform to the expected. Like the friendly man of my childhood, we have ceased to posture and to distort our features in social rituals. We are free to wear our new, real face. I must not forget another freedom because it is vital to our peace of mind. That is the freedom from worrying because we can no longer help others.

Looking back on the landscape of life presented in my retrospection, I recall with a heightened appreciation of my family's Provincetown beach cottage when the last day of our summer vacation had arrived. The water had been turned off in the house, the storm shutters were fastened in place, and I was released from any obligation to plant or weed until next season. It was still early in the day, and I took a final walk on the beach before heading for the car. It was only then that I saw the beauty of the dune grass and the bayberry bushes, that I tasted the soft tang of salt in the air, and felt the sting of wood smoke from some beach barbeque. I sat quietly on a dune to enjoy the expanse of tawny sand and jade-green water shimmering with brilliance. Having freed myself from the daily chores, I had gained an appreciation for the beauty of nature around me.

In the difficult period, which I likened to the neutral position between car gears when we had not quite let go of the old ways nor mastered the new, we often worried that we were useless. We could not be trusted even to babysit for our grandchildren any longer, and our help with carrying dishes was often a disaster. As for aiding the family with gifts of money, that too became impossible for we soon found ourselves in the category of incompetent, with someone else holding our power of attorney.

For us, this condition is not a tragedy, but a release and a blessing. We have learned about giving and receiving and where the benefit lies. Our lifelong schooling has taught us that the help we offer is not always received with the same pleasure that we enjoy when giving. In giving, we become the person who wants to give. This is our growth. What we can offer now is the aggregate of ourselves. We can extend infinite patience born of the new time that we experience now. And we can give the kind, all-inclusive love, which is the flowering of understanding and wisdom.

Looking back, we wonder at the importance of the daytime. We were like children, always active, doing something. We dreaded when the parents called us in from our play to go to bed. "One more minute, just one more game."

Now, among our freedoms is freedom from daytime activities. For us, bedtime has become a most delightful moment. We anticipate the feel of the sheets, the warm blankets folding us in against the chill, the pillows upholding our heads on the sea of sleep. It is then that we let our whole body go. The stiff muscles relax into utter comfort while the night extends before us with all its stillness. We never freed ourselves from bonds that, like shackles, impeded our progress, nor did we turn away from the concerns of our friends.

One fine day we wake up to discover that the old world has disappeared. It is not there any longer. We have jettisoned the preoccupation to nourish ourselves on warmed-over scraps from other people's living, to pretend an interest in trivial scores along with all the tiring smiles and head noddings. We do not miss, nor do we want the freedoms attached to the conventional wisdom that bonded us to temporal judgments. All the secondhand interest that filled our lives—like Mr. So-and-So's trip to Greece or Mrs. What's Her-Name's talk at the club, or the cute remarks of someone's grandchild—has left from our attention. The old bondage to accept ways of acting and reacting loosens of itself and falls away.

We are like people on an ascending escalator who feel like they are standing still. Their hands are on the railing, motionless, as the floor recedes beneath them; yet, they are ascending.

What wonderful guidance life gives us—a slight shove here, a gentle pull there, a hint, a whisper! We have completed our course in life. And now, with nowhere to go, we move to the still center of our Being and discover an entirely new world with plenty of living to do.

Never think we have assumed a sour-grape attitude, hiding a series of losses by calling them freedoms. We have lost nothing. We are moving from an elementary reader and simple arithmetic books into inspired literature and the pure mathematics of tomorrow.

ON THE TORTOISE PORCH

This morning I was thinking about the two tortoises on the tortoise porch. Years ago, when I got the tortoises, I kept a chair on the porch for human use. But the tortoises were forever becoming lodged between the rungs of the rocker, and I had to pull them loose and remove the chair. The furnishings, after that, included a large sandbox, a shallow bathing pool, which was once a Chinese copper tray, and a cave-like affair made of boxes under which they could crawl for sleeping. I sprinkled the floor with sand and lettuce leaves—all tortoise décor.

I thought about the tortoises this morning because they have taught me much. In our latter years, we bring into the present episodes which were once meaningful. We conjure up animals because of their immediate, instinctive response to the laws of life.

Many of you have pets, but I doubt that you consider them teachers; few adults look at pets that way. The unquiet, active phase that you live in now seldom gives you the time or awareness necessary to gain this knowledge. We watch these gentle, silent creatures as they go about the twenty-four-hour job of being themselves. Through them, we recognize life's pattern of diversified oneness, which make up the laws of nature.

We review the mistakes we made when we thought we could live as independent individuals. Like the tortoises, we took the long way around. The tortoises had no choice. Their will could not go contrary to their nature. Mother Nature upholds them in her care, directing them in all their ways. She dictates what they can eat when they must seek water, or start across the warm desert on their spring explorations. Our ears have lost the power to hear Nature's maternal voice. We learn by painful, often tragic mistakes.

We eat anything at any time. With control of light, we destroy the natural rhythms and make our dawn and sundown. We are free to make mistakes, but there is one thing about which we are not free—desiring our good. We make curious errors about what is good, and, having failed once, we try again and again because making "good" is always our goal.

But to return to the tortoises. They are of the desert variety. I received one of them seventeen years ago from an old Cahuilla Indian at Thermal in the Coachella Valley near Palm Springs. The other one I found wandering around on the terrace. The shell, the carapace, is twelve inches. I am told they grow very large and will live to be a hundred years old.

The first thing one remarks about the tortoises is their extreme slow motion. We call to mind the fable of the tortoise and the hare. We remember that the tortoise won that unmatched race despite its lack of speed. And we also know the reason. The tortoise knew where he wanted to go, and he kept on going there. He had persistence and a sense of direction.

I have often detected this sense of direction and persistence in my tortoises. On warm summer days, when the mock orange scent is strong in the air, and the Copa de Ora vine reaches over the porch wall heavy with golden bloom, these cold-blooded creatures lust for travel. As they start across the porch, heading east, I have turned them around and around in the opening ritual of the game of blindman's-bluff, then placed them heading in the opposite direction. They have always slowly turned themselves back and begun again to move toward their aim.

When obstructing events turn me away from my course, I think of the tenacity of the tortoise in advancing toward his goal. I recognize how vital this oneness of purpose is, and how necessary perseverance is to reach a goal.

As humans, we are goal-oriented. We are born with the urge to strive toward a goal that, along with our physical growth, we are not conscious of it. A goal gives purpose, and without purpose, there is no reason to get up in the morning. The beautiful and bright light of a new day is not enough.

From the tortoises, I also learned the wisdom of an unhurried pace. They can take their time because they have many winters to chill their blood for the long, underground darkness of their sleep. They have many summers of the desert sun and warm sand to heat their blood into activity again. Their actions are timed for a long continuance.

In the late autumn, when the nights turn cold, the tortoises eat less and less of the green leaves of lettuce and Swiss chard. Finally, they even stop drinking water. Their motions, always slow, become even more sluggish. They seek the corners of the porch for their sleeping cave and draw head and legs under their carapace. The next morning, they are not misled when the warmth of a winter sun abated the chill in the air. They know that their cycle of rest has arrived—when the life of all tired things returns to its roots for renewal.

I observe their preparations and know that the tortoises prepare for hibernation—that five-month-long sleep. I place them in a box and cover them with crinkled paper, tucking it around them and over them to simulate being under the earth, as they would be if they had dug their sand tunnels in the desert. Then when the time for their resurrection dawns, I will hear them rustling the papers with the first, slow emergence of the limbs. They have awakened into a new life but are the same old tortoises. Well, not the same. They have grown new. They are nearly a half-inch longer than when they "died," and any scars of living, such as a bitten toe, have healed.

The hibernation of the tortoises and the preparation they make for it are nature's way—her gentle, merciful way—of putting her children to sleep.

When my mother began to settle into the sleep that carried her into her new spring, she too wanted to eat less and less, and finally wished nothing at all, not even water. I would ask her if she was hungry or thirsty, and when she showed that she was not, I remembered the way of the tortoises and did not urge her. She was obeying the same compassionate directions which had guided them. So deep had the lesson gone that I refused to make an inquisition into life's ways. I would not use feeding tubes and medications to make a nightmare of her first gentle dreams. As it was, she moved so imperceptibly into her desired bedtime that I was not sure at what moment she fell asleep.

UNDERGROUND RIVERS

In looking about for analogies in nature that will help you understand us, the rivers of southern California come to mind: the San Luis Rey, the Santa Ana, the San Gabriel rivers that go underground during the long season of no rain.

On the surface, the rivers are dry, without the faintest tint of green marking their border. The tule rushes are gray and bent. Only the lacework of many wrinkles on the riverbed shows that a stream once flowed there. Were it not for the high bank and the water-rounded boulder, one would find it difficult to follow the course. These dry riverbeds are like our bodies—dried up, parched, and wrinkled. But underground, the rivers flow in all their fullness, deep, silent, and purified. They no longer carry the silt of disturbed, shallow water, and discarded trash does not float on the surface. The underground water is clear and refreshing. Deep within us, too, life flows purified and quiet. We have finished with the ceaseless activity of the churning white river.

We now move through an inner, calmer channel. You could sink shafts of communication to this fresh, sweet way of life filled with peace and understanding. In the middle years, you see only the surface and cannot fathom what lies beneath. It satisfies you to meet us at the level of the riverbed where little sustenance flows. There is a time for all things, and this is our time for rewards.

As we look back to your phase of living, which was once ours, we see all your connections moving on the surface. In our reality, we are invisible to you. You cannot see us growing in depth. And we cannot communicate to you, in words, what we feel. It is a small wonder that we are incomprehensible to you. Like the rivers, we have gone underground to a place where we use a secret form of communication.

Turning from the analogy of the rivers, I shift my attention to an aquarium of the little fish on my bedside night table. I use this now to show how we are free to travel as far as the heart desires while still confined in a tiny space.

Often in the night, when I am not interested in sleep, I turn on the light above the fish tank and fancy how it would feel to swim in clear water, or to rest suspended, almost motionless, breathing through delicate, fanning gills. I spend many hours watching the fish. I enter their watery world by using my imagination to identify with another form of life. I swim between the green water vines and above the iridescent shells watching my shadow rift over the sandy bottom, foreshortened, and then elongated by the light ripples. I become a small fish in an aquarium. I make this world mine.

The world in the fish tank is restricted in space as much as the world of life's graduating seniors. We live in cramped quarters. But these restrictions are necessary to learn something of the mystery of finite space and how we may conquer its limitations. Mother Nature teaches us through her children, the fish. Many of us cannot get far on walking. Walls of one building or one room, perhaps the four corners of a bed, restrict our world. But this space does not have to limit us any more than it limits the fish. As I watched the little guppies and identified with them, Nature, our mother began to teach us how to cope with the problem of limitations.

One must be humble to become a little fish. With awe in our hearts at the wonder of life, we turn to the guppies. They have learned that the glass wall that encloses them does not limit them. To avoid contact with the barriers, they swim in smooth circles. The fish adapts to their limitations from experience and observation, as we do.

I remember reading about a whale that had not learned this. It had been captured for Marineland at Palos Verdes in California. As soon as it was placed in the tank, it began to swim in a straight line, dashing headlong against the wall. Divers went down with it and directed it around in circles. But the moment they left the whale alone, it again swam in a straight line. Before long, it had killed itself in a hopeless fight against its limits. The other fish, in the same tank, swam endless miles in a circular course and never came up short against the sides of the aquarium.

I also have learned to move in circles. I do not push against barriers and wear myself out. I have learned to avoid them by not going where I know I cannot go. I live as if the space available to me is as vast as infinity. I am like the little fish who swims in the open sea as far as the setting sun and, yet, never leaves the confines of the aquarium. I need my confines. I cannot walk one mile, and having lost that ability, the desire to do so has also gone.

I doubt any of us in the senior class desires to play a game of baseball or run in a track race or dance all night. It is pleasurable to recall such activities, but we would not find them amusing anymore. Even the so- useful outlets for energy cannot interest us. Such action as polishing the car or working around the house seems not worth the effort. Our activity is an energy that flows from thought to thought rather than from place to place and rests at the still center of our Being. No matter how appealing a picnic with the family may be, we find it tiring. The noise of many voices and the turmoil of clashing interests leave us fragmented and scattered. The many demands on our attention and memory confound us. People around us are familiar, but we cannot recall the names that go with the faces. We sense your impatience caused by our forgetfulness.

How much more pleasant it is to lean back against a comfortable pillow on our bed, close our eyes and be wherever we wish—and with the speed of thought. There, we meet with those we want to see and hold conversations with them without interruptions or misunderstandings. What we say is always clear, and we are quick to understand their point of view.

In these thought-contacts, we are closer to our friends than when they sit next to us occupied with other interests. We may sit across the table from each other and, yet, be separated by an ocean, for they may be intent on beaching a small craft on the opposite side of the earth while we dream of a campfire under the sequoias.

These thought-contacts are available to us now that we have gone underground like the rivers. You have noticed our lips move, heard murmured words, and have thought we talked to ourselves. We did not. We were having a delightful dialogue with a special friend who lived extremely far, as space measured by train or plane, but was as close as our own heart.

We are like the San Luis Rey River, the Santa Ana, or the San Gabriel, whose dry grasses, shifting sand, and tumbled, broken rushes cover the gently flowing, cool water. And there is not even a trace of moist earth, not one green blade to give away the secret.

WEAVING A NEW GARMENT

How destructible our bodies are! How soon the physical garment wears out! It is this wearing out process you notice first about us. Our presence reminds you that, if you live long enough, you too will go to pieces, and that disturbs you.

Our hearing becomes uncertain. Some of our hearing loss arises from our lack of interest, for we often hear a great deal of no interest to us. Our eyesight, too, is wearing out. Why not, after all these years? We have listened to all that is worth hearing and have seen everything worth seeing. We are tired of hearing what our ears can hear and tired of seeing what our eyes can see. We often refuse to wear the hearing aid and misplace the glasses you bought us. We do not wish for louder hearing aids but better things to hear. We do not want better lenses to see with but better things to see.

Remember, we are growing new. We emphasize that we are not losing anything, but are gaining new and finer faculties, which make the old ones obsolete. Why should we hold on to an old, dated garment which has become too small and uncomfortable for us? We do not blame you for your concern with our fading senses and useless faculties since, in your world, one could not survive without them. We want to get rid of them.

Our only concern with falling-apart is the trappings that still cling to us. We ask you to allow us to slip free of them altogether, that you permit Mother Nature to let us change our garments in her own wise and gentle way, just as she has assisted us with our earth garment.

Because we are so concerned with the body, we have allowed the old one to come along as best as it could, with only the instincts to guide it. That is why we so often act like small children. You say, with a kind tolerance, that we are in our second childhood. But you are referring only to our childish behavior, not to childlikeness. To be sure, we act childishly because we have lost interest in directing our bodies. We have let them go, and now only the most primitive instincts guide them. They work on their own volition as though they are not a part of us. Our mouths may consume an entire box of candy at one time without being aware of it until someone calls attention to this chocolate orgy. Our hands may play with our food. We are careless and awkward and spill things. Our toilet manners are less than desired, but our bodies now are like those of little children and should receive the same patient care, the same loving help.

Lack of function of the self is not responsible for our present childlike actions and the feeble working of our brain. The brain is only an instrument that is part of our tired body. It is worn out, perhaps damaged. We might think of the living self as an orchestra always playing and of our brain like a radio that makes the music audible. An old radio wears out the tubes, and the resulting music sounds cracked, like an old voice. People say that the music is cracked. But in the radio's case, the fine orchestra is still there, behind the corroded wires and decomposing wood. What we hear is the disintegration of the chassis, which impedes the full output of character.

Nature shows us the chick discarding its shell when there is no longer any need for it. We see the butterfly leave the cocoon behind as it soars into its new dimension of a summer sky. The shell and the cocoon have served their purpose. Our bodies, with their tired brains, have also served their purpose, and we are far too busy to be conscious of them. We are at work on our new garment, giving it the finishing touches.

A Familiar Place

I am turning again to small pets to learn all that I can from their instinctive ways. We have many other sources for acquiring this sort of knowledge. The trees of the forest have much to reveal to us, with their mighty strength emerging from a small beginning. The sea and mountains are also splendid teachers. They are not accessible to most of us now, but we can visit them by instant thought-travel—a means of transportation that needs no care, or train, or plane, but which carries us to our destination with less bother.

But the pets around us are very natural teachers. The little parakeet that lives in the cage by my window has a broken wing. Other parakeets would have killed him in the aviary. I like to think that by taking him to live with me, I saved his life. I called him Pagliacci because of his clown-like antics. He hangs upside down from his swing-perch, enjoying an inverted view of the world, and then drops to his head. I must confess that I have failed to discover the lesson inherent in either of these habits. Though the meaning of the clowning still eludes me, Pagliacci taught me the importance of having a safe place to live—a familiar room, or even just a bed.

I became aware of the importance of the familiar as I studied the little bird. I imagined how it would have fared had it been forced out into the world. It would not know where to find seed or water. It might fly into the glass window and break its fragile neck or fall prey to predatory hunger. And if he tried dropping on his head from the ledge of a high building, the descent would mark the end of his topsy-turvy world. Then I began to apply the bird lore to us, and I wondered how we ever could have been so foolish as to think of the walls that surround us as restrictions of our liberty. With us, as with the bird, the purpose of a cloistered place is not to keep us in, but to keep hazards out. Does little Pagliacci feel grateful for his protective bars? I have no way of telling, but when I take him out to clean the cage, he is impatient to return to his familiar security.

At the summit of our years, we experience something of the same sort of restricting and enclosing that the bird undergoes. The garden where I sit on a pleasant afternoon, enjoying the shade of an umbrella, often faces a busy street with a rush of traffic and many pedestrians—all of them strangers—going heaven knows where! And between me and all that restless activity is a chain-link fence with a locked gate.

We sit in our lawn chair and wonder what it would be like if we could walk through the gate and find ourselves on the other side, jostled by strangers—when our equilibrium is uncertain, at best. Or how would it be if no fence protected us from the accidental skidding of a car across the sidewalk and into our sanctuary? Or if no locked gate prevented the strangers from coming in and helping themselves to the chairs under the cool blue-and-white umbrellas. Thinking about such possibilities, we learn the blessings of an enclosure. So, we have no desire to wander off to strange places where anything might happen.

Do not distract us from our studies to acquaint us with our new environments while we prepare for our final examination. We need our concentration to move safely among unfamiliar objects in unfamiliar rooms. Walls of a new color make us feel as though we live in a different element. The shape of a new chair draws us toward its newness. We are not at home around strange contours.

In our familiar room, we are at home, even in the dark. Our outstretched hand always meets the doorknob. We do not need to interrupt the peaceful journey of our thoughts to think where it is. Everything is where it has always been. The firmness or softness of our old bed and pillow are as intimately known as our skin. The slight depression in the mattress fits the shape of our body.

At night, when the lights are out, we can reach toward our bed and find the glass of water or the Kleenex tissues, or whatever we need, because we know where it will be. Knowing where a thing is releases us from giving our attention to it.

Once I took my son's cat, Touser, to spend some time with me. He was no longer a young cat. He had become accustomed to my son's house and garden and had set up a domain familiar to him. Touser, in his later years, had become a very composed and contented cat. In his environment, he kept a lofty and detached attitude. But the moment he entered this new house, here on the terrace, he stood in the center of the living room, and his tail jerked and shivered.

Slowly, crouched low, he began the rounds of the different rooms. Upstairs and down, he explored the possibilities of attack and of protecting himself. At the least sound or sudden movement, he would leap straight up in the air. When he ate, he did so apprehensively, and he refused to go outside even to investigate. The inside was a smaller piece of the unknown. Several days passed before Touser calmed down, and several more days before he began to enjoy the pampering he was receiving. All of this because he concentrated his attention on becoming acquainted with the new place.

I felt sorry for Touser. If my son's absence from the city had not made the change unavoidable, he would never have been uprooted, even for a day. Uprooting is a traumatic experience for all living things.

One of the most tragic appeals I have heard was from a beautiful woman who had just arrived at a new rest home. As she was being helped down the hall, she murmured, "I want to sleep in my bed. I want to sleep in my bed." I can still hear her quiet voice stating a fact she knew was irrelevant. Whoever she was, and wherever she is, I am dedicating this chapter to her.

How important it is for us to be free of all distractions to devote our remaining time to change from the old ways to the new ones! Do not move us about as though the change from one room to another, or even from one bed to another, was a small consequence. Perhaps the move is best for all, but the resulting gain does not compensate for our loss. After a move, we feel like some poor shell creature pulled out of its protecting cover and lying exposed to all the dangers. We must find our way back into our inner peace all over again, and this we cannot do at once.

When we are thrust into an unfamiliar world, we must learn anew where everything is. And learning about our outside environment—a task we should not have to repeat at this late day—is very tiring. Our interest is not with it, and we resent that use of time.

Last Sunday, my daughter bought her mother-in-law, who was in a convalescent hospital, a new handbag. She was careful to buy one that was like the old one. It required much gentle coaxing before the mother-in-law would allow transferring the contents of the old bag to the new one. She insisted that the old bag served her well, even though it had a broken strap, and the clasp no longer held.

She could not say she did not feel at home with the new bag—that it did not feel right for her. Her fingers, which she could no longer control, knew the way to hold the broken strap. It would take a deal of energy to get used to the new one—a very tiring effort demanding concentration.

Nature shows us the chick discarding its shell when there is no longer any need for it. We see the butterfly leave the cocoon behind as it soars into its new dimension of a summer sky. The shell and the cocoon have served their purpose. Our bodies, with their tired brains, have also served their purpose, and we are far too busy to be conscious of them. We are at work on our new garment, giving it the finishing touches. It may be challenging to grasp the importance we give to the warm, dear object that brings us comfort. Family members and professional caregivers must have sensitive and compassionate hearts to understand our concerns.

When our lifelong companions have gone on before us, and we are alone, you advise us to sell the old home, which, you remind us, is too large and a burden. We have spent precious years in the old place with someone we loved. Every inch of the old place is grooved to our ways and is warmly familiar. Every friend who has shared with us this space, which we call our home or apartment or room, is still there in spirit. His presence is perceptible everywhere.

Every scratch on a piece of furniture is like a story in a treasure book. When we notice the scratch, we smile, remembering who made it and when. We would not polish it away for all the world. The twisted handle to the refrigerator door reminds us of a dear companion who caught hold of it to prevent a fall. We will never get it repaired. No sanding machine will erase the moment and the glow of happiness that arises when we see the stain on the hardwood floor and remember the puppy not yet housebroken.

We realize why it is so difficult for you to understand what you call our stubbornness in wanting to remain in our old surroundings. You emphasize that the new apartments are bright, cheerful, and convenient—nothing to carry out and everything easy to dispose of. And you assure us that we can make new friends. You have many sound practical reasons for moving us to someplace better suited to our reduced physical abilities.

We hear your persuasive arguments and your well-meant attempts. However, we cannot present our reasons for wanting to stay where we are. Our brains are too worn out to function that way. If we could, we would like to remind you that despite our appearance, the time we have left is precious to us. We have our whole life to review and to understand, and we are also receiving intimations of the new life we are approaching. We are transferring over to another circuit, to a more rapid vibration. We need a peaceful, uninterrupted time in which to carry out this change. We should be free to move through the well-worn grooves we have made, which we can find without redirecting our course.

Please be patient. Do not hurry us. When the time arrives for falling asleep, we will loosen our grasp on the familiar objects of our own accord.

ROUNDED STONES

Some of you have had the fortune to travel to the country. Maybe you have spent your childhood there, where every object of nature reveals something about life. Nature slips her instruction into our reveries in the guise of a rooster with his harem of hens, or a horse in a panic, or a leaf falling, or a flowing brook.

As a child, you must have felt the fascination of a brook—the clear, cool water winding along the edge of a pasture, and the smooth, rounded stones that covered the brook's narrow bed. You watched the stones as the sunlight shifted over their pale surface, imparting a wavering glow. They appeared to be rippling and undulating in a light-and-shadow water dance. But, more likely, your main interest in the brook was to catch the crawfish that hid under the stones and would dart away, leaving a cloud of water-dust when you moved a finger. As an imaginative child, you played at being a crawfish, or a water baby, and experienced the thrill of living in a little cave-house in which you could hide. Minnows, too, were in the brook, but they moved too swiftly to catch. All you could see was their shadow flashing over the sunlit stones on the bottom.

Then there were the stones. With so many colors—some were iridescent like pearls, some had a pale olive color, and others were a dark blue-black. Occasionally, a broken piece of bottle-green glass lay among them, as beautiful as any emerald. And the roundness of them! There was a fascination in that roundness. Many ordinary stones lay about in the field through which the brook found its babbling way. But we were not interested in these. We would never think of collecting them or carrying them around in our pockets. They were rough and had sharp, cutting edges that could hurt. But the smooth, rounded stones were different. They felt good in our hands, and we rolled them between our fingers. Certain ones were charms. We knew at once which ones had this unique property. They would bring us good luck, and we could do many impossible things with the power they gave.

The quality of smoothness gave the stones their value. As children, we never thought much about the smoothness nor what makes the stones smooth. We responded to their smoothness. We believed they were different and valuable.

In the early spring, when the brook had thawed and flowed clear as glass in its bank of tender green cress, the swiftly running water tumbled in the channel. If we could apply feelings to stones, we would imagine this as a very disagreeable experience for them—stone against stone, hitting, scraping, tossing. And always the sand on the bottom acting as an abrasive, spring, summer, and autumn, scouring away their surface.

Throughout the spring, summer, and fall, water subjected the stones to the smoothing process. Not until the winter's cold slowed all nature to sleep, did the stones rest motionless in the clasp of the frozen water. Congealed in ice, they waited for the coming of another thaw when their perfecting process would begin all over again. Season after changing season, the brook went about its business of rounding the stones until no part of them protruded too far from their center. Nothing in nature juts out too far from its center. Too much would work against the protuberance if it did—the force of gravity, rain, wind, and the irresistible urge to knock it off.

We, of the graduating class, are like these stones. Our lives have known many changing seasons, and all of them have contributed toward rounding off our sharp edges, doing away with our aggressive extensions, smoothing us into polished people. Not all the smoothing comes by an external process, though. Attention is a life-giving force, and as we draw it into our essential center, the core of our being, the spurs, spikes, and barbs on the outside wither away. When the season for sleep comes, plants and trees draw back their sap, much as we draw back our attention, and leaves, which have served their summer purpose, turn gold or crimson, and fall to the earth.

When you think about us and understand how we differ from you, you will know how compact and rounded our inner, invisible form has become. No part of our character thrusts out sharp and brittle challenging attention.

Life has not spared us much. Year after long year, we have weathered many elements and been tumbled about. Difficulties have scored us with their abrasive blows. Periods of freeze have numbed us beyond our ability to react. We could get nowhere. We could not make effective decisions, to change an unprofitable business, to seek a new location to live, just as the stones could not move when in the grip of the frozen stream. We had cut loose the combative ties and withdrew ourselves into a stupor, our hibernation through the season of non-action.

We have wasted much energy fighting our constraints, forgetting that there is a time for all things under the sun. We abandoned ourselves to the natural rhythm, the stream of events flowed over us again, and life took up its work of smoothing our rough edges—our unpleasant, sharp aggressions.

Living in close contact with people, no matter how much we like them, is a trial. It is life's way of removing the cutting edge of our personality, of buffing away the splinters. Nature teaches us to rid ourselves of the barbed retort or suffer the barbed consequences. We learn to do away with our small, pricking eccentricities that have fomented turmoil. Our desires are not unequaled in the universe. We try not to irritate by reciting lists of complaints. We compare ourselves to our neighbors and realize that no one escapes difficulties in the school of life. Difficulties are the problems set for us in this textbook. Each day we turn a page and find new ones waiting.

Rounding and polishing do not make us like two dull peas. No child has ever found two stones alike in the brook. Each one has, besides its roundness, its unique contour, its particular color. The white stones, so translucent that we like to think of them as agates, have their slight variations, their delicate suffusions of rose or ochre. The green stones run a chromatic scale from a gray olive to pale chartreuse. Even the smoothness differs according to the substance that composed the stones.

We no longer need to be exposed to the swift waters of life, and we are through with being tumbled and scoured. I once heard that when you learn to live in a house, you can tear it down. I would also suggest that once you learned to live with people, you have earned the right to be a hermit.

Many of us have receded into a sanctuary within ourselves. This aloneness is ours by rights. Long years of rubbing shoulder against shoulder with our fellow men are the coins that bought our present, peaceful solitude, and now we can rest in the small bend of the stream, away from the swift current, for we are like polished stones gleaming through the still water, rounded, and smooth.

Link by Link

As we review our life to prepare for the unavoidable final test, we see the pattern of each event, like a colored tile that completes a mosaic. If one tile were missing, the design would be incomplete. Everything we have experienced is necessary for us to be. If we had not made one friend, not taken one turn in the road, we would not be the person we have become.

It is interesting to trace back a treasured friendship to its beginning and discover the first link in the chain of events that brought it about. A link implies that there is another link further back. We randomly choose one and call it a beginning.

I tried this link exercise in tracing my career as a sculptor. I went back to an afternoon when a poet on a walk around the terrace stopped to admire a flowering pomegranate tree in my garden. He knew that I had written some poems and invited me to select some to read at his home, where he held poetry readings each month. I accepted. Each of these events was a link. If I had not gone to his house, I would not have begun to sculpture again. Had I not studied sculpture many years ago, I would not have been prepared for what followed.

At the poet's house, I met a woman whose son was teaching a class in ceramics. I was only slightly interested in ceramics, glazes, and all that, but since the young man had just started his class, I thought it would be helpful to join. As part of the course, I made a figurine of Brother Lawrence, known for his "Practice of the Presence of God." On the strength of this one piece, I received a commission to do a life-size sculpture of St. Robert Bellarmine. After this, I received commission after commission, and all because a pomegranate tree was flowering in the garden.

Link by link. Every one of them was necessary and, therefore, good. We regret nothing. As we rest in the conclusion of our life, in the completeness of our design, we are grateful that we have learned from the mistakes we had made. We do not think, "Oh, if only we had not done that!" If we had done any differently, we would not be the person we are. It is unjust for the person we are today, with our present knowledge and wisdom, to pass judgment on the person we were years ago. That other person did not receive the lessons we have learned over the years.

We cannot do other than what is good for us. We have no free will about this. We lack maturity, education, judgment, intuition, love. So many lacks! We make many errors in learning what that Good is. We make judgments and take imprudent risks; we make mistakes and fail—all because of ignorance. But how are we to learn if not by trial and error? There is no free will in this as much as there is no free will in a toddler learning to walk and falling many times before he succeeds. Failure itself is a lesson, and the urge to try again and perhaps fail again drives us to take another risk but always with the hope to evolve the concept, gain knowledge, and possibly succeed. If we suspend judgment and take no chances, we make no mistakes, but we remain ignorant. If success is impervious to us, maybe we paved the way for someone else to succeed and, in so doing, seal our legacy. Would Johannes Gutenberg have been as successful in inventing the printing press were it not for the few that tried before him? The battery we use today to power our modern contraptions evolved from a stack of copper and zinc discs invented in 1800 by Alessandro Volta. He, too, learned from the success and failures of those who came before him.

Link by link we reduce our ignorance and increase our knowledge. Step by step we fall and rise to reach the ultimate Good, the good of the self, our whole consciousness, or spirit, or whatever else you would call that mystery at the center of our being.

We know that everyone wishes to reach the Good, that ignorance causes errors that will result in failure. "Ignorance" and "mistake" are ancient words that have been discussed throughout the ages by the wise and chary, by realists and idealists, and by many others. On the other hand, Long ago, we forgave them for their ignorance. But to forgive ourselves was much more complicated—pride blocked forgiveness of ourselves. We fancied ourselves foolproof. We could not tolerate making a mistake.

We had learned to forgive our mistakes by the time we reached the graduating class. We learned not to expect the impossible of human nature, not to e judge nor denounce anyone. We move in an aura of peace.

Everything has a purpose. And every splinter of the link depends on something other than itself, even though we may not see with our physical sight. We cannot easily trace back the sequence of links as I did with my sculpture, but it is there, nevertheless.

Seeing is not necessary for knowing. We know much that is still a mystery to our rational thinking and much that the eye alone cannot verify. All we see of a tree is the trunk, the spreading branches, and the vibrant pattern of leaves. But we know that a great underground root nourishes the tree. The tree could not lift the curve of its branches nor hold them against the onslaught of an autumn gale without the support of the unseen root— the link with the earth.

Or we might picture a sanctuary lamp like those found in old European churches. Upon entering such a church, we are at first aware of the cool darkness. After the brilliant Mediterranean sunlight outside, our eyes are blind to the rich details of the interior. But as we become accustomed to the shadowy dimness, we see the faint glow of a lamp hanging from a long, linked chain above the high altar. We cannot see where the chain is fastened to the vaulting above because the darkness receives those links and shrouds the others in mystery. We can see only the lamp and the links closest to it that receive its light.

If we were told—no matter by what authority—that there were no links except the ones which we see, and that no staple fastened the chain to the vault above, we would not believe it. We would know that the lamp and the visible part of the chain could not hold themselves up like the rope in an Indian rope trick. That we cannot see the rest of the links does not bother us. We know they are there, one attached to the other with no break until the whole length of the chain is securely fastened to the vault. We need no faith to accept this—our reason tells us it is so.

We can easily apply the analogy of the lamp to our own lives. Our years in this world are like the visible links in the chain. The links that continue beyond our mortal sight; they are the life that lies ahead, mounting upward until it reaches that which upholds it, and has always upheld it and will uphold it forever. We do not need faith to accept this truth concerning our lives any more than we needed it to accept the truth about the hanging sanctuary lamp.

There was a time when we had no leisure to wonder about the continuity of our lives. We treaded on a wheel orbiting around an active center. We began each morning more driven than drawn toward the work of the new day. We gulped a cup of coffee as we watched the clock, then drove like mad to meet the challenges that waited for us. We had no quiet moment at the beginning of the day in which to orient ourselves, to reaffirm our purpose of living, to restate our overall goal for the unit of time, which was this Monday or Tuesday. Instead, with no greeting for the morning, we found ourselves on a wheel that went nowhere, carrying with us all our confused tensions and frustrations.

Is it any wonder, then, that we are thankful for our release from the wheel? We no longer return in the evening, again fighting the traffic, too tired to question the purpose of this life, too indifferent to wonder what all this activity is for and where it leads.

Now we can question and evaluate. Now we can think about the hanging sanctuary lamps that may still need their continuous chain and about the magnificent mosaics in which even the smallest tile is essential for their completion. We can think about contingency.

What a limitless subject contingency is for our meditations! It means belonging and depending on all things as all things depend on us. It means infinite extensions of ourselves through all creation.

It means link within link, hand in hand, heart to heart.

BEYOND THE WITHERED LEAF

We have arrived at the anteroom of our life. We no longer direct our energy to our bodies or mental activities. We have no use for the reasoning faculty of the intellect. In this grade of learning, we need only the intuitive faculty. We must be detached and serene to receive the revelations of our intuition. To hear the still, small voice of our instructor, we must enter the hushed center of our being. We concentrate our attention on a center within us. The harsh sounds of the outer world startle and hurt our sensitive hearing like a clap of thunder.

We examine the image of life in our sensitized way. We listen for intimations to come. Contact with the loud, busy, and flashing world is unpleasant, and we avoid it whenever we can. What companionship we may still need, we find in the muted life of small, slow-moving animals curled asleep on cushions, or in growing plants.

Some of us have a plant growing on our windowsill, or a sweet potato in a glass of water. We watch the emerging bit of life and meditate on the gracious ways of Existence and Being, which considers the small potato necessary in the scheme of things. The leaves reach up and unfold in the air, not down in the water, where they would rot. The roots do not lift into the air to dry but descend into the water, their proper element. The plant does not know what part to force down or raise. Science has names for this process but tells us nothing about causes—about the mystery in which we are about to take part. We are now able to grasp this mystery through the revealing light of intuition.

The plant we keep on the windowsill grows toward the light, and the leaves always bend in that direction. The flowers, when they blossom, lift to the sun. We experiment a little. We turn around the flowerpot and notice how in a day or two, the groping leaves have adjusted to the changed position and again reach for the light, their source of energy.

Conscious awareness of your own Source of life is essential. The battle of life leaves little peace for wondering, scant leisure for questioning how the plant knows where the source is. When we practice to still our minds and move inward to the center of ourselves, we descry a life-giving of giving the love that is in every created thing. It is the Existence and Being that nourishes us and draws us to Itself as surely as the sun draws the plant. But for us, with our earth limitations, the source dwells within the heart.

When I turn from the indoor plants and see the amaryllis that grows outside the dining-room window, it, too, reveals a way of growth that applies to us. In the sequence of the amaryllis, the leaves appear first. In the spring phase, the leaves are young. They shoot forth in the form of green spears, aggressive-looking, and full of push. But before long, the green leaves lose their stiffness. They grow yellow and wilt. Their grand challenge lies upon the earth, useless and ready to throw on the trash pile.

The amaryllis's life is like ours. When you see us stretched out on our beds, or sitting in a wheelchair doing nothing, do not take it for granted that there is no purpose in our living any longer. We are in the stage of development of the wilted amaryllis. Our bodies are bending back to the earth. We are tired. But the story of the amaryllis is not over. The wilted leaves, far from being useless, play an essential part in the plant's life. The strength they garnered from the sun and nurtured with spring rains flows back into the bulb to give sinew to the life to come. An ignorant gardener, with an inappropriate passion for neatness, is likely to cut off the wilting leaves and impoverish the whole plant. He wants everything just so and in order—his sort of order. Some of you may feel that way about us. In your passion for order, you make things difficult for us. You interrupt us when we rest, reviewing our days. You break the silence we need to hear the faint teaching because, in your world, meals must be served on time, and sheets changed at a certain hour. Everything must be in order—the gardener's sort of order.

But the plant has its order, too. While the stage of the wilted spears is not spectacular, it is vital to the plant. An underground activity is going on beneath the yellow leaves as it is within us, hidden from the world.

All the good we have gathered in our green days, all the knowledge and wisdom we have collected through the long summer of our life now move inward to nourish us in that secret place where we now dwell.

When the year ripens into fall, and the warmth of summer rises from the edge of the earth, the shriveled spears of the amaryllis prepare for the harvest, sprouting from the bulb the gorgeous, pink blossoms into their undeniable beauty. From the amaryllis, we have learned that flowers follow the withering of the spears. We have learned the sequence and accept the dying of the plant.

We are in the season of the yellow leaf, and a gracious purpose is at work within us. As we feed a living harvest back into the core of our life, the flowering will come.

A magnolia tree in the front garden taught me a variation on the theme of the amaryllis, spear, and blossom. Early one evening, as I was placing the hose for a long, slow watering of the tree, I noticed that the large, glossy leaves were turning a rust-brown and curling slightly. Already the ground was strewn with them. In the evening stillness, I watched one leaf and then another toboggan to earth through the air. I glanced up at the dramatic, ivory-white beauty of blossoms, cushioned on rust and green cluster of leaves beginning to unfold. If we could see only the leaves, we would believe that the tree was drifting into its fall slumber or that it was dying. But the flowers tell a different story. They are a climax of loveliness—the rarest beauty that a tree can produce—a wonder of how earth and root and the trunk could bring forth such enchantment of color and texture. They glow in the twilight as though they are translucent and lit from within. The flowers blossomed when the leaves reached the end of their time, and the tree seemed to die.

Our sequence is the sequence of the flowering tree. We do not see the entire picture when we look upon the fallen leaves. It might be difficult for some in the undergraduate class to see us as triumphant blossoms against the sky. You focus your sight upon the earth, fixed where the fallen leaves lie. Our flowering hides from you because it belongs to our next phase of existence. It requires perception to be aware of it.

But if you know where to look, you may discern the dim outline, the faint glow of burgeoning growth. For instance, an elderly man who wanders about the rest home asking, "What shall I do now?" over and over again annoys you. He will empty the wastebaskets or take the screens out of the windows. So, you find some activity for him. But once he has completed that, he again asks the eternal question, "What shall I do now?" Once, he may have been self-centered, he may have accepted the help of others with never a thought of returning it. His senseless repetition is the withered leaf of a summer that is over. The blossom may be there, too, longing that the man contributes his part. If so, this wish of his is now blossoming forth. Do not let the idleness of an older man deceive you. Remember, you see only the fallen leaf. His accomplishment is in himself, in what he has overcome and in what he has become.

Or consider an older woman who goes about the home removing clean sheets and pillowcases and consigning them to the soiled clothes hamper. You find this habit annoying. No amount of talking will divert her from this practice. She looks up at you with her soft, childlike smile, as though you were praising her, and waits for the opportunity to strip the bed again.

Think now of the rust-colored leaf, turning and drifting through the still air until it comes to rest in the long afternoon shadows that stretch across the lawn. Changing sheets that need no change is the fallen leaf. The older woman has no intention of causing trouble. Her wish is to do her part—to keep busy, helping in any way she can. Her desire is a flower unfolding.

But even if you find it impossible to see in us the achievement beyond the withered leaf, it is there, and we know it is there upholding us, giving us warmth and comfort, and great inner strength.

With One Word

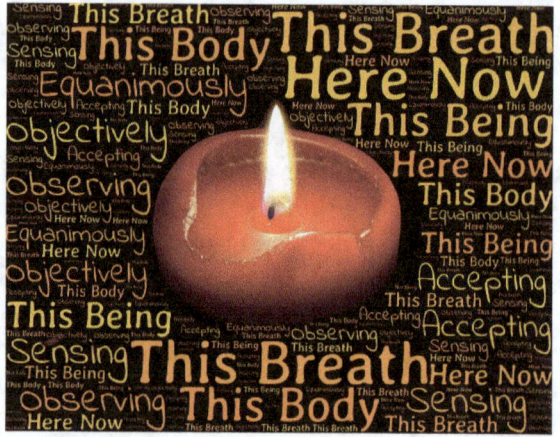

Some days, we are too still to think about anything or to remember even the happiest event. You may consider these our bad days. You whisper to someone, "He isn't very alert this morning, is he?" Or "This is one of her withdrawn periods." And that someone looks toward us, shrugs, and gives a wry smile to show some pity.

These gentle days are a time of quiet growth, like flowers with their petals spread out beneath the sun, drawing in strength to continue living. We are in contact with the source of all things we call Existence and Being. We make that contact through our breath, being conscious of the rhythmical drawing in and breathing out.

You are not aware of breathing unless you are a guest of the water world, or you exercise in the thin mountain air. But with us, sometimes we are aware of nothing else. Nothing about us seems alive except our breath, and nothing else appears to move. The tides ebb and flow with the changing seasons, the procession of the vernal and autumnal equinoxes.

Men have always known how to use this rhythm to expand their consciousness. In ancient days in India, they repeated a holy word, such as "om," or the name of a chosen deity, as they inhaled and exhaled breath. A monk at Mt. Athos learned to use his breathing as a form of unceasing prayer.

Life has taught us how to use this rhythm. In a moment of stillness, after the doors of our senses close, and we doze at the root of our Being, we hear the word "Love" repeated over and over. It flows as a sound from within us. We do not recognize it at first. Gradually, we find it with our breathing. "Love," whispers our exhaling breath. Then we move into a state of stillness with intent, listening for the word with our every breath. We become fascinated with this simple repetition, its basic rhythm, and the word love. Great power is building within us.

Just as man learned to harness the natural power of a waterfall to generate electricity, or the inherent power of the wind to turn a windmill, so we learn to build up this concentration of love from the gentle rhythm of our breath. If we had a rocking chair, we would rock to the rhythm of this word. If we could walk, we would adjust our footsteps to the beat of the word.

Love is entrenched in us. We breathe love, our life energy, which comes from that Existence and Being—the source of all love. As we exhale, we send forth the love we have received and direct it to some person or situation, or the four corners of the earth. We do not dole it out or withhold it from those whom we once sat over in judgment. We are through with judging. Our love falls like the sun and the rain, over the just and the unjust, for we must pass on the love we have received. Love is like a flowing stream of sweet water, which would stagnate if not propagated. Circulation would cease.

We, of all people, know about circulation. You are always urging us to exercise to keep the blood circulating unobstructed. The flow of love is far more critical than that of our tired blood. It is a balance between the love received and the love given, and we find no difficulty to keep this balance because we live according to the law of nature, the law built into all creation.

During these latter days, it is a splendid experience to direct love toward a troubled situation and watch it go to work. For instance, one morning, the nurse comes into our room. With our eyes closed, and even before she speaks, we feel the tension and irritation that hold her tight as a rod. The woman across the hall had refused to allow her to enter. Her room, the woman insisted, was her castle. The nurse expressed to anyone who cared to listen to her opinion of older people and their castles.

Now we turn our attention to the "Love" word. We repeat it as our breath flows in and out, feeling it permeate the room and the overtaxed nurse with its relaxing warmth. The nurse is still muttering to herself while we feel love moving out from us like circles of light around a streetlamp on a foggy night. The whole room glows with the feeling of love. As we send forth our love, we feel it replenishing, so we are never empty but always filled.

What an exhilarating feeling it is to give to the just and the unjust! To give like the rain and the sun. We know there is no one—not the irritated nurse, not anyone—who can carry her little heartfelt of darkness into our light and keep it there. The light of our love will also expel their darkness, for that is the marvel of light and love everywhere.

"Love. Love," whispers our breath, and the surrounding people appear, not in the darkness of our fallible judgment, but in the light of our love.

We have this love with us, for we could not live without it. Our first waking breath says "love," and we become conscious of its warmth, blanketing us with infinite security. In the quiet of the evening, as our breathing slows into the ebb of sleep, we give ourselves over to safe keep the mysterious course of this love.

With love, we rest in peace.

Enough Is Enough

No one will continue to drink from a cup once emptied. A person will relinquish the cup, thankful for the cool liquid it once held and will not try to squeeze out more when there is no more.

We, in life's graduating class, have extracted every drop of nourishment and refreshment in the various levels of our experience. Some of this experience was a bitter brew. We learned how to mix the bitter brew with the delightful, savoring each new concoction, and learned from it accordingly. We are not about to return to an empty cup for our sustenance. We live in the accumulation of our experiences, gathered, and centered.

Like the sedimentary mountains formed by weathered rocks, we are formed by the drift of the years.

Our present is like a photograph album collection of our scenes from infancy to the present day under one cover. All the pictures are with us now. We can look at them without going back. But the time has come to close the book for good.

Our lack of interest in the past is not a bad sign. Like all the changes taking place in us, it is part of growing new. How often can a person remember himself as a proud six-year-old holding his first baseball bat or react with pleasure to that birthday episode? How many times can one relive the tragic death of a friend and find tears to shed? Or feel a thrill at the thought of an old love experience, no matter how much it once meant? A hundred times? A thousand?

No more can a sunset flow across the sky or the grass turn violet with the fallen blossoms of the jacaranda tree and still rouse us with its beauty. A time comes when old stimulants no longer stir a response within us. In place of an ecstatic "Ahhh," we murmur, "So what…?" The most beautiful music becomes an interruption—a noise that shatters the beauty of silence. Color fragments of pure light and the shattering prism tire our eyes.

There is no lecture, no concert, no party of interest to us. We have already heard all the words we care to hear. We have seen all the colors and forms and have made all the contacts we need in one life. The mere strength required to go anywhere is exhausting.

On some mornings, when we wake and see our shoes waiting for us beside the bed, we find it almost impossible to go through the motion of putting them on. If we wore a pair of shoes all day, by our seventy-fifth birthday we would have gone through this same motion fifty-four thousand seven hundred and fifty times. Is it any wonder that on some days, we would rather not get up at all?

Youth is a potentiality, a possibility, a promise for the future, and the middle years are taxed with the weight of responsibility and anxieties. We learned all we could from being young. We think about the young as a book of blank pages. Someday, when the pages have been written, and the reader has found a story of wisdom or blunders, the book will be rewarding. But by that time, it will be a book about age, not youth.

As a child, I enjoyed reading a book on aging. Somehow, I knew that the furrows which mapped the face of one about to graduate from this life were honors earned. They were marks from the Great Teacher showing a work well done. The shining though vague image of my grandmother still illumines my third birthday. She is with me here, in the present now. Sometimes she lifts me to the hall table and ties a bonnet under my chin and calls to my aunts that they must not go for a drive without me.

And sometimes a wise and ancient Scotsman, who entered my life when I was twelve, joins me here and now. He had been the target of a tease for the neighborhood children. They carried his porch chairs into the street and left his garden hose running. He had begun to dislike all children and met them with a full blast of the hose.

I remember the overtures of friendship I made over the garden fence as I tried to break through the barrier of mistrust he had raised between himself and all the children. I remember the companionship which grew between us as we came to know each other and learned that we shared a mutual interest. For he was a Scottish poet, and I had always loved poetry. He used to read his poems to me from a volume with a cover that looked old-fashioned even then, with its wreath of heather and titled *Nuggets of Gold from Memories Mine*. I have forgotten the poems, but I still recall the stories he told. They opened before my imagination a new country of crags and rolling mist of Bothwell and Stirling castles and the forest of Glenfinlas. From him, I learned of the story of William Wallace, the hero in the eponymous epic poem by Blind Harry and protagonist in Braveheart, portrayed by Mel Gibson, and of Robert the Bruce, King of Scotland in the early thirteen hundreds, the warrior who had fought successfully for his country's independence from England.

The neighborhood children urged me to play with them. But kickball and hide-and-seek could not compete with the romantic history of early fourteenth century Scotland or the poems under a wreath of heather.

I went to school for the first time when I was twelve. I had no idea what the proper pupil-teacher attitude should be and broke all precedents by finding the teacher the only interesting person in the classroom. She had not lived as long as my Scottish friend, but as children measure time, she had lived for a long while.

From this woman, I learned much beyond the courses listed in the catalog for Miss Gordon's French

School for Girls. I saw the beauties she had seen during one sabbatical year of travel in Italy. I saw my father's birthplace through her eyes as she talked of standing on the hill by an old castle looking down on the curving blue bay of Castellammare di Stabia where my father used to spend his young summers.

I did not know then that my classmates would think my friendship with this teacher was the most brazen apple-polishing. I had not heard the expression "apple-polishing." But I could not be concerned with the standards and taboos of the children. I longed to brim with all the beauty of the world and all varieties of experience. And I realized that I had begun to fill the vacuum of myself.

Youth possesses an immense store of energy— enough to last a lifetime. But this is only physical power, neither good nor bad, neither wise nor unwise. It is like the wild spirits of a young fawn as the April snow melts on the Sierra Nevada mountains of California, and a brilliant exuberance patterns their spring dance. It is like the energy of salmon leaping up the Columbia River rapids in exquisite silver arcs.

But we have no desire to try a spring dance nor a salmon-leap. We no longer need this energy. Not for anything do we wish such activity. What strength we had served its purpose. Now we experience the inflow of another sort of power meant to serve another need. This new energy is more like light than motion. It glows and illumines the sanctuary within us and draws us to its magnetic core. We are through with the activity caused by physical energy, not because we give up on it but because it is through with us. There is a delicate balance when the object of our interest recedes from us and we lose interest in it. The receding and loss of interest appear simultaneously.

I recall an episode that I like to have with me in my present. It includes my little boy, me, and a summer in Provincetown.

I had called him to come up from the beach where he was playing. I had been making molasses candy and wanted to give him some. I watched him winding his way through the clumps of eelgrass, both hands extended and having difficulty keeping his balance. Bobby was a tiny boy, and walking was still an adventure. When he stood before me, I saw that he was holding in each hand several precious, sandy shells. For a moment, he eyed the candy I was holding out to him, then his gaze turned to the cache he had found. I followed his thoughts. He could not take the candy until he had relinquished the shells. His eyes moved from the prize in his hands to the candy in mine. He placed the shells aside and brushed his hands off for the desirable sweet.

While he was eating the candy, I turned the incident into a little parable. People who like shells better than candy would say that he had lost the shells, but people who like the candy better would say that he had gained the candy. The boy had to choose between shells or candy. The exchange of shells for candy was better for him.

What we choose to discard in life differs for each of us, according to our inclinations. What is not different is the fact that we cannot receive more than our cup can hold. And we have had enough.

We have walked barefoot through life, reacting to everything: the chill dampness of dawn-wet grass, the warmth of sunbaked sand, and the sharp edge of stones. We shouted with pleasure and cried out with pain. The pendulum of our days swung between extremes, and we called the thrill of it "living." We wanted to be where the action was, and we swung between pleasure and frustration, between big dreams and deep despair. We did not know that there was rest at the fulcrum from which the pendulum swung. Had we known, we might not have been so interested in the wild extremes of emotions. The time has come when we have had enough of the opposites of life. And just when we knew that we had had enough, we discovered that our feet had become so calloused that we were not aware of the chill grass or the sharp stones any longer. When we were through with the pendulum, the pendulum ceased to swing.

There was a time during the retirement community period when we feared that soon we would have no friends left. So many of them had gone on to the next level of living. They had left us feeling very much alone. And we dreaded being alone. We tried to get a new friend for each old one who had gone. Occasionally we succeeded, but more often, the additions remained just acquaintances whose names we were always forgetting. Seeking friends was a habit. We realized this when we had no energy left with which to look for them. With the loss of strength came the realization that we did not embrace friends anymore. A visit with them drained us of our meager energy, and their goodbyes left us exhausted.

We have so much else that is entirely satisfying, so much that gives us a joy and security, which are this day's bread.

We have had friends—a whole life filled with them. We have had a lifetime filled with about everything. What experience did we not explore to the depth or climbed to the heights in our time? What part of life could we wish to repeat?

Enough is enough.

Exchange for the Better

From time to time, I overhear my friends whisper how much I have lost. They express pity for my loss of various faculties and functions: hearing, sight, memory, balance, and, sometimes, indecisive or muddled talk. I forget people's names nor know today's date. I misplace my reading glasses too often, and I must hold on to the arm of the chair each I get up. I pretend not to hear. While there is some truth to that, it is also a fact that there's much I pretend not to hear, see, do, or remember.

We have graduated from the school of life and now retreat to the special place at the center of our Being. We require peace, quiet, and repose. The bustle and babble around us are obstacles to a smooth journey. We no longer need to make choices and decisions, nor do we need to take an interest in the here and now. The present has meaning to you who are in the full bloom of life and have a future ahead of you. We are in the withering stage of life. Our future lies in the hereafter. Only our distant memories have meaning.

No doubt, you remember how it was when you graduated from one grade to another. Early in your life, you transferred the pleasure of beating the highchair tray with a spoon to beating a drum with drumsticks. You exchanged your colorful painted kindergarten equipment for first-grade furnishings, and so on up the line of promotions. You traded kickball for high school basketball. You always exchanged outworn, outplayed things for newer pursuits.

Once you delighted in shopping in toy stores. To you, they were veritable treasures-houses. You advanced from balls to toy trains, and on to Meccano sets and bicycles. Or if you were a girl, you went from soft animals to dolls and dollhouses, to skates and bicycles, and then to clothes—always exchanging one interest for another. The progression followed your growth.

We give up much that we considered valuable for something greater. Events such as grand openings, or parties, or traveling no longer interest us. We look forward to the non-events of a peaceful evening in our room and the joy of lying in our comfortable bed.

Higher powers have taken over. Our eyesight is dwindling. The outer world visible with our physical eyes is diminishing, and we turn our vision to our inner self.

Soon we will see far more than meets the eye. This inward vision is beyond the imagination of the juniors at the school of life. They must wait to graduate to our class to see the splendor that opens before us.

My mother, in her last years, could see her new vision beyond the limits of the physical sight. An optometrist would have said that her eyesight was about gone. Yet, how she could see! And not only see but see-through. Her ken guided me, although it was not apparent to my younger eyes. Today I see it as a privilege to have had intimations through her vision of what to expect in my late years.

The same exchange occurs with our hearing. The noise and clamor of the world grow faint. We give away the ability to hear with our ears for another sort of hearing. And what exquisite music comes, as in a dream, from the music that Beethoven heard when his ears had grown deaf! What ethereal fancy Matisse created from colorful paper cut-outs in the years of his fading sight!

Muted remembered voices whisper to us; they warm us with their love, assure us of their presence And before long, we hear that small voice, audible only when the sounds of this world have grown silent. Soon we hope to make a significant exchange—the exchange of our worn-out bodies for new ones.

Our bodies are like a car. We identify ourselves with our cars. We say, **m**y horn is loud, **m**y spark plugs need changing rather than the **car's** horn, the **car's** spark plugs. We feel assaulted if someone collides with our car, and we express our aggression with throttle and screeching tires.

In the same way, when **our** body is tired, we say that we are tired, when **our** body is hungry, we remark that we are hungry. We even speak of undesirable conditions with a strange possessiveness, referring to a cold as **my** cold. A headache is always **my** headache. We are the operators of our body, just as we are the operators of our car.

For a long while, the car filled our needs. But after a time, it deteriorated and developed idiosyncrasies. The brakes misbehaved on the road, but we controlled its shenanigans by shifting gears, even when they were slipping, and we made a note of the amount of gas or oil needed because the gages failed to work anymore. We got along with the old car. It reminded us of the many good times we have had, of so many delightful trips. We were used to it.

But the day arrived when we had to go somewhere, and the old car refused to start. Only after many attempts did we catch the sputter of the engine turning over, punctuated with coughing, spitting, and backfiring. The headlights were dim, and the battery was too far gone to recharge. Still, we kept the old contraption. Besides, the garage mechanic had said something about carbon deposits. He also remarked about a car not lasting forever. A time came when the car stalled and refused to start again. We sat in the car and said to ourselves, "The car is of no use to us anymore." We know that it cannot be repaired. It has not been of any use for a long while, and we could never depend on it again. Instead of carrying us around, we have been pushing it. There is no reason to sit here any longer, away from everywhere, in this broken piece of machinery. Then we took our energetic selves out of that old car and walked away without a backward glance.

Soon the tow car will come and haul the wreck to the junkyard, but we will not be in it. Of that, we are confident. We will not be in it.

We are on our way to get a fine new car.

NOT ABOUT LONELINESS

Loneliness is a most dreaded condition, like a climate of gray and dreary weather over the future. You think we are lonely when you see us spending much time alone. Don't. From our summit, we can see that loneliness is not something real. We have learned the truth about it, and it has set us free.

Loneliness can best be understood by comparing it to something like it—something like darkness. We experience darkness, too, and, yet, darkness is not something real. It is a not-ness, a not-light. We cannot measure the speed of darkness nor follow it to its source as we can with light. All the studies in the world cannot teach us how to manipulate darkness to make it disappear. There is no way to turn it off by using some property of darkness itself.

To cope with darkness, we must think about light. If we know the quiddity of light, where we can find it, and how we can bring it into the darkness, we solve our problem. To banish the dark is to introduce the light. Darkness cannot exist with light. Where does it go—that darkness—once we have introduced the light? Nowhere. It is never anything. It does not go into another room. It does not add itself to the total of darkness because it never existed as a thing. It is merely a lack of light. We, who live in the summit of life, have learned that loneliness, like darkness, is a nonentity.

In our transition period, when we reconcile ourselves to playing a senior citizen role in a retirement community, we grope around, hoping to escape the gray fear of loneliness. We join a group because we do not want to be alone. We surround ourselves with people as insurance against loneliness. As we wean ourselves from the traditional way of evaluating friendship, we reach out to some latent capability.

We deal with our lack in terms of a lack, dispelling darkness with darkness. But before long, we learn that this method accomplishes nothing and makes us feel even more alone. We learn that new friends do not replace old ones. No epoxy can fill the void of a shattered cup. Emotional incompatibility clouds the relationship between one person and another.

It takes a life's learning to see that the only place where one is not alone is at the center of one's self, the center of our equilibrium, the point beyond the flux of this world. There, at that still center, we are complete. All that we require is the realization, the awareness that within our true self, we are whole and invulnerable.

To find this still center, we need our creative imagination—the one faculty that we possess to explore the unknown, to go beyond anything we experienced before, to venture into new realms. As we continue to focus on our inner center, we feel the love, the light, and the warmth glowing within us, and we learn where Elysium is and where it is impossible to be lonely.

Most of us will arrive at this place; it is our foreordained destination. Loneliness helps us on our way because we cease trying to cope with it as if it were something in itself and begin to think of it as we think of darkness, a not-ness.

Feeling alone is a dis-comfort, and like any other discomfort, it is a warning. Just as dis-ease informs us that something has gone wrong with our ease and prompts us to discover what it is and to remedy it, so should any sort of unhappiness prompt us to search out the reason for it.

We do not need to look far before we discover that we are hungry for love—not the fleeting, romantic love, not the changing, exciting sex experience mistaken for love, but something entirely different.

The time comes when we no longer have the physical energy for romance. That is when we begin to feel loneliness. But we are not alone. We are like the little boy who had given up his shells to fill his hands with candy. Instead of dealing with loneliness by rearranging our lack of friends, our lack of love, or by pretending that we are not lonely, we turn to the source of our completeness, the source of love.

The love that is present at the center of ourselves—which is one with Existence and Being—begins to make itself felt. We are aware of its presence within us not because of any words we have read, nor because we have tried to believe in it, but because we have experienced it.

This essence of Existence and Being marks the finest period of our lives. It is that hour in the garden, in the cool of the day when that which we have imagined in various forms and called by multiple names walks with us.

We are not alone.

Drawing from Life's Saving Account

For many years we have planted, watered, and weeded our garden. We have done the work, and now we reap the harvest of our wheat-gold season. The seeds we have sown and the care we took of them tell us if our harvest is lean and of poor quality or gratifying and plentiful. From the summit of years, we see the growing conditions of the seeds we have sown and the character of their growth. We can make do with poor reaping if we know what caused it. The harvest shows us which seeds are good and which had better be left unsown. The yield shows whether we cultivated assiduously or inadequately and whether we allowed useless diversification to crowd out essential growth. This knowledge is useful when the time comes for sowing again. Now, in the wealth of our fall, we reap the fruit of our labor. We toiled through the best of the day, and now, in the evening's coolness, we rest.

Rest is possible for us because you have assumed the responsibility for our care. You supply shelter and food. Such care is a financial burden. If we have been able to put enough money aside to cover this period of dependency, we are fortunate. But even if we are not a financial burden, our care is always a restriction on those who attend to us. We are aware of the evenings when you would like to go out but do not, the trips you cannot take because it is impossible to leave us, the parties you dislike giving at home with us about.

We try our best not to be demanding, and we lie long hours in a cold room before we call for another blanket. We color your life as much as a child would. Our bodies have returned to the ways of childhood. You do not resent the intrusion of little children, but sometimes we feel that you resent ours. We understand how we could be a burden. But either from love or from a desire to keep our dignity, we wish to pay our way.

Then a time comes when we receive the wisdom to understand that we have already paid. The concern falls into perspective. We paid in advance. The time of graduation from the school of life is our season for reaping. Once there was a season for sowing, and we sowed. Every thought or action is a planted seed.

We made our contribution at the time for contributing. Once we were an executive or a worker, a teacher, a physician, or a homemaker. Whatever we did, that work was an investment toward this hour. It may not be apparent that we did anything or added to the knowledge or culture of our day; nevertheless, by just living, we deposited concern, energy, and love in the bank of life. And to have lived long, we accumulated many riches. Our bank account shows a healthy amount to our credit, more than enough for our present need. Our investments are paying off.

During our early years, we invested in the love we gave our parents, brothers, sisters, and friends. Later we invested in the community in which we lived by showing interest in its welfare and growth. We rented or bought a house. We mowed our lawns and planted flowers for all to enjoy. We helped with school affairs and assisted neighbors. Or we were a "character," adding light and color to the stodginess of conformity. We were one piece in the mosaic that made up the town without which there would have been a gap in the tessellation.

We are not about to downgrade ourselves with false humility. We see our achievements with a clear vision. We invested in our children. We could not add up all the doctor's bills, the bills from the orthodontists, the bills for clothing, food, and schooling—not to mention what we spent in anxiety and always in love.

In those days, we gave unconditionally from the fullness of our love as easily as we breathed. All parents did. We never added up the bills. We never counted the cost of anxiety and the havoc it could have caused to our health. We forgot the sleepless nights when a croupy child awoke well in the morning. Sacrifice was never a word we used for depriving ourselves to give more to the children. Sacrifice is a noun that does not apply to free and loving care. The law of life controls the balance between giving and receiving, sowing, and reaping. This law is always in operation. We know of it through science and religious teaching. We bury it in our memory like the words of an old song which we have forgotten.

But now we recall this balance. It assures us that we will receive as we have given and encourages us to bring out the old bank book and to notice the many entries over the years. It elucidates the law itself.

Our lesson is to learn the art of receiving graciously. Many of us are still awkward at this. We protest much. Sometimes we outright refuse to accept a gift proffered in kindness, grumbling something about the old handbag still being useful, and push the new bag away. We do not realize that we are ungracious. We wish that we were giving you something instead of receiving it. It does not come naturally to many people. But when we have learned the balance between giving and receiving, when the truth of this law is a certainty and not just the words of a motto, we receive graciously. By accepting, we give worth to the gift and the giver, and we earn his affection. This receiving is an art.

One problem connected with giving and receiving, and which hinders our paid-up status, is that those who take care of us now, may not be the ones who owe us anything. They may not be our children or friends. Their tending to us may not be a direct return for anything we could give to them.

When we think of life as a bank, we are no longer troubled by this apparent unfairness. No one expects to draw from a bank the same checks or currency they deposited. The money we had deposited was stamped in our bank account. Then the bank used it for some immediate, pressing purpose. Later, when we come to withdraw the funds, we are paid in a different currency— one not deposited by us but by someone we never knew.

The bank of life functions the same way. We read to a lonely person. We do a favor in our business or professional capacity with no thought of recompense. The deed is noted in our deposit book by the laws of symmetry, balance, sowing, and reaping. If we believe that the harvest should yield interest, then something less than copacetic motivates our deeds, and our return will be something less than rewarding.

We withdraw what we need. The return for having read to a lonely person may be in the form of insight into what loneliness is. The business or professional help we gave may return in the gratitude that we see from our window—an autumn tree in all its glory of gold leaves.

We seldom receive the same gift as we give, but the balance equals the amount given to the same returned, and we are wealthy in all that is fundamental and essential. Should we not stay here long enough to deplete our savings account, we can change it into a traveler's checks to be cashed at some future date in the country that lies ahead.

THE BEQUEST OF LOVE

There was a time when we hoped to leave our loved ones a modest inheritance. We dreamed of how pleasant it would be if we could secure a future for a wife, a husband, or a child. We would have liked to enrich our friends, too, with gifts by which they might remember us, that might ease them over a difficult time or enhance the enjoyment of a pleasant one. We imagined our beneficiaries going to the bank to cash a dividend from a gift of some stock we had left them. We saw them pause as they endorsed the check, and we knew they were thinking of us with loving gratitude.

This childish dream is a leftover from the kindergarten level of life's school. We now know how fleeting memory is, how transitory. Alas, we know that no number of gifts can buy a loving memory. We also know that we cannot leave you any real security from life's experiences. To do so would mean withdrawing you from the school of wisdom.

Looking back over our life and that of others, we saw how the most careful planning or the keenest foresight could not protect a foolish wife, or husband, or child from his or her foolishness.

Security rests in the possession of a wise and understanding heart. To attain wisdom and understanding was the wish of young King Salomon, who went to the high place of Gibeon to ask God for the gift of wisdom and knowledge to serve his people. At his young age, he knew that we could not come to wisdom and understanding by wishing, nor could we leave them to you as inheritance, nor teach them to you or impart them by example. We must reach them through our efforts.

What can we bequeath to you then? What do we have of lasting value? What gift is priceless, cannot be frittered away, and will last forever? The answer is love. Love fills all those problematic requirements. It does not become obsolete; it is beyond price, and it cannot grow any less. Love is for eternity because it is another way of trying to name Existence and Being itself. Besides, it is ours to give and yours to keep. We can leave it to any number of you, using a mysterious system of division that does not diminish. For love is like the flame of a candle, which gives its light to other candles without reducing its fire. In the same way, the limitless source of our love will never be lessened, no matter how much love we bequeath.

Love provides a warmth more satisfying than a mink coat, which we might wish to leave our daughter. The memory of our love can armor our children with acceptance and assurance, which will give them a sound footing for as long as they live. Love left to a house can brighten it so that it will continue to be a home glowing with a warm welcome long after we have vacated it.

What we remember and cherish most of our mothers and fathers, our relations and friends, are not the material possessions they have passed to us, no matter how valuable they may have been or how grateful we were for them. Material things go out of style or no longer fill the needs of our future. And money has a way of disappearing.

But love never becomes old-fashioned, or square, or unneeded. How often have we brought into our present some special moment that held the love of a mother, or father, or a dear companion and warmed ourselves with that bright glow when the world appeared gray and cold? In our sheltered rest, we find sanctuary in an old love that is forever new. Often, I bring into my present the good loving night, which my father always wished me before I went to bed. I hear the gentle, Italian words with which he gave me over to God for safekeeping. *Amor di Dio, proteggi mia figlia*, he said. Love of God protect my daughter. What a legacy that was! And the look of love in my mother's eyes in the last few months of her life, when she could not express herself in words, is worth far more to me than any annuity. Love received is a wealth that never adds up to a given amount. We cannot add love to love. There is no mathematical symbol for love.

Now that we have all this leisure, we consider the gifts of love that we intend to leave not only to those we love and not in exchange for anything but freely, as the sun gives its daily light and as the rain falls.

If the ones to whom we would give our love live far from us, we can write to them or call them if we are able. If not, we can send them our love by thought waves. We can broadcast our love to them wherever they may be. Have you ever found yourself thinking of a distant loved one, wondering how she is doing and soon after receiving a phone call from her or a postcard? You marvel at the coincidence and say, "I was just thinking of you." But was it a coincidence? From our inner center, we can send forth love in rays that travel outward like ripples from a pebble dropped in a still pool. We can send love to warm and comfort everyone on our wavelength—to all those tuned in to our station of love. We see ourselves as a broadcasting station for love.

Now that we have received the gift of leisure and are released from the whirly world of activity, we see that people everywhere need us. They are bogged down in the merry-go-round and cannot get off. Not yet. We delight in sending the warmth of love to ease their passage to the next level of life.

Our ability to send forth love in this way is not just a sentimental fancy—something dreamed up, imagined. We can test it in the laboratory. Our brain waves are electric—thought is electric. It goes on continually and can be intercepted by a sensitive receiving instrument. In a scientifically controlled experiment made in Pasadena, one person was thinking of a dog, and another person, sitting in front of him, received the imprint of the dog on a piece of sensitive developing paper, which he held close to his forehead. As science advances in knowledge, we may explain this phenomenon in different ways, but what happens will remain the same.

In ancient times, when a man heard thunder, he believed a god caused it by hurling his great bolts across the sky. Now we have other ways of explaining thunder. What is important, though, is that thunder still goes on happening regardless of our understanding. And so will the transference of thought.

Some of us will always experience a sudden knowing of what another person is thinking. We will expect a visitor to receive an unexpected phone call from a friend with whom we have been conversing mentally. No matter what is the current fashionable explanation, the power is there, and it is ours to use. Our shortcomings need not make us feel useless. We need not lie in our beds, gazing at the ceiling, and feeling sorry for ourselves. There is a far greater gift to give our progeny than money or babysitting the grandchildren. We have love to give.

When we practice our ritual of love-sending, we go through various steps to vitalize our creative imagination. There is no set way. We use whatever viable steps we find. The actions I use in my ritual of love-sending are these:

1. First, I follow the rhythm of my breathing, repeating the word "love" either aloud or mentally, relaxing the rhythm of my breath.
2. When I become relaxed and engulfed with love, I see myself as a lighthouse and my heart as the great light.
3. I beam my ray of love out into the vast, dark loneliness.
4. I turn the light to the North, to the West, to the South, and the East.
5. I stand on the four corners of the world. Sometimes I see some desperate man, a lonely heartsick woman, a misunderstood child, and I feel a sense of peace and love blanketing them—people I have never known out there where my love has reached.

Once the love-sending has become a habit, we no longer need to go through the ritual of the lighthouse, or whatever aid is most helpful to get us started. Some of us prefer the broadcasting station, and we do not always send without a specific target. Often, we beam our love to one person or situation and behold the astonishing result in the form of an unexpected postcard or a phone call or simply feel the warmth of an embrace.

How wonderful it is to contemplate the infinite amount of love available for sending—the endless amount that is ours to bequeath!

The inheritance of love, which we leave to you, requires no administrator, nor any bond, nor is it subject to gift or inheritance tax, and neither can the most utter foolishness of our beneficiaries ever squander it.

Sorting for Tomorrow

We have arrived at the time of sorting. We have been sorting all along, but now there is an urgency to rid the buildup from years of living. When we appear to be rocking and humming to ourselves, we are engaged in the business of sorting. We are a bit squirrely in our instinct to hoard many things against a time of need that seldom comes. Many objects with which we burden ourselves never fulfill their promise of "coming in handy" someday. Many contacts which we thought profitable proved worthless. And all this cache has been mounting for a long while. Because we once found value in an experience or idea or held on to a trivial relationship, it does not mean we should continue to do so forever. That value may have belonged only to the needs of our youth.

Some of our memories have lasting value, and we should keep them and bring them into our present whenever we long for the comfort derived from reliving them. But I am thinking of those fragile souvenirs, the little flatteries, and praises that helped us overcome our young lack of confidence. I am also thinking of the petty hatreds, dislikes, and judgments that we held onto through the years. All such clutter takes up room we cannot spare. One advantage of moving from place to place, from one level of consciousness to another, is that we tend to the business of sorting. We do not understand how many useless objects, or memories, we have accumulated until we clear the top shelves.

It will not be long before we start on our journey to the Great University for our higher studies. We must separate the things we take with us from the things we leave behind. If a memory is still alive and warm with love, then we should place it to one side for packing. The love-filled event, a revelation of wisdom, must be kept. The thought of our childhood home or the home where we lived when we first married, these memories we hold. But all the dusty mementos, which ceased to be a part of our growth, will go on the throwaway pile. We take nothing that weighs us down. We want nothing of bad taste or foolish when we unpack our belongings for our new life.

We will mark "To go" all the love we have received throughout our earth years and all the love we have given. Even the harm we refrained from doing counts as an act of love. The unjust remark to which we did not reply, the blame we took upon ourselves to save another from difficulty, we pack these expressions of love for our final journey.

We will also take our sense of direction, the faculty, which records all the paths we took to our destination. The first independent decision we make marks our point of departure to life's journey. We meet many unexpected delays and take turns that send us off course to experience adventures and misadventures. These are essential in life's journey. We see that now, with our inner sight, they are the off-scripted chapters in the school of life.

We cannot communicate just how wonderful it is to appreciate our total experience. This appreciation cannot be examined through a course of studies as one would study art. The artistry of it all must be experienced—the good and the bad. It will come to you when your growth is ready for it as it came to us. One day you will descry that knowledge, and it will fill your whole consciousness.

Oh, yes! This sense of direction toward our goal is something we will take with us. It is our passport to travel—our ticket marked with our destination. The Travel Agent has arranged our journey and our reception when we arrive at the other end.

Since we want to leave no unfinished business and no loose ends behind us, we need to learn what to do about the heap of discarded and unwanted rubble, which we wish to be free of forever. How can we dispose of all the bitterness, the prejudice, the urge to injure, the love of flattery, the false-faces we wore, the pride, and hypocrisy? What shall we do with them? Life does not want these blueprints to be found and copied by others.

We learn what to do with the discards when we move into our phase of sorting. It is as simple as all magic formulas. The alchemy requires the power of love full upon the pile labeled "Unwanted." When subjected to love's radiance, evil ceases to exist.

Love acts upon the memories we wish to discard as white dye works upon a dark garment we want to bleach. We place the dark clothing in a vessel filled with hot water and pour the white dye. The garment becomes white. Where does the color go? It has not gone into the water. The water is as clear as ever. By the process of chemistry, color has ceased to exist. Forgiveness acts on love like white dye on dark garments. What we forgive, we forget.

Many errors cease to exist for us now. We pour the forgiving love upon the past mistakes and watch them disappear. We sit in our wheelchair or lie on a bed gazing at the ceiling while turning our love and understanding upon the discarded errors.

We plan to leave nothing dark and ugly to stand in the path of those who follow us. We take nothing dark and sinister with us to the splendid dormitories where the Perpetual Light will shine upon us.

We beg of you. Do not demand our attention for some small detail in a pattern that no longer exists for us.

We are sorting for tomorrow.

THE CITADEL WITHIN

In the terrace behind my home on the hill is an acacia tree that the wind blew down a few winters ago. It split the trunk but did not break it entirely. It curved to the ground in a lovely arch, forming a natural chapel in the forest-Gothic. The tree has continued to live according to its legend of perpetual life year after year, sending forth its feathery green leaves.

I come to this shrine early each morning to tune myself to the vast orchestra of life and to offer my day to further a purpose necessary to my understanding. Although I do not know the overall purpose, it gratifies

me to know that there is one. No words are used in
offering the day. A person does not express his awe in
words on seeing a majestic scene as the snowcapped
volcanic upthrust of Mount Shasta against a blue sky.
Instead, he experiences the breath-taking moment
silently while something passes between him and the
grandeur of the mountain that words cannot describe.

For much the same reason, neither do I use words in
this moment of offering. But I need to use words now to
communicate what passes inside me, between the small
part and the whole. Words like this:

> *"Here I am, a little microcosm, drawn by love to the
> great Macrocosm. Here I am, a creation of love,
> drawn to Existence and Being. I offer myself and all
> my actions to further the plan of creation. I desire to
> be a channel and a tool for the Great purpose."*

Then, in the same way, I take my physical body to
this place, I move inwards to the secret citadel at the
center of my being.

Within us all is a citadel, a still center where
Existence and Being dwells. It requires a quiet period of
introspection to reveal itself, and we, who have lived
long, have had the time to find it.

We find this secret place by using our imagination.
With imagery, we explore the realms where our thoughts
have never gone before. Scientists, inventors, all make
use of it. I remember one evening standing outside our
home with my father, who was an astrophysicist,
watching a shower of falling stars. My father asked me to
imagine what could cause a star to fall. I was a small
child then, seven or eight years old. He did not expect

me to come up with an original theory, but my little brain started working that way. A friend of mine, a patent attorney, made a small fortune because he imagined that if he were a dog, he would like his food to look like a bone. He created and patented the first bone-shaped biscuits. We must turn to our Being to find this realm of imagination. A whole new world opens to us once we have dwelled in it—an understanding of things once thought impossible becomes yours forever.

Once we have learned about this wonder-working faculty, this creative power within us, we put it to work expanding our field of consciousness. We begin with the body, sitting with our eyes closed, breathing gently, rhythmically, until we become relaxed and still. Then we quiet the mind that is watching our thoughts dart from one subject to another like a bird hopping from branch to branch. And then we discover that we are not thinking the thoughts. The mind feels the thoughts as though they are separate from us, like a wound clock ticking without help, or like the bird flitting from branch to branch. We watch and observe.

As we watch our thoughts, we notice the way their restless motion loosens. They become slower and slower to an eventual stillness. When all is calm, we focus our awareness on our heart or solar plexus, the still center. After a while, we feel a warm glow like love or light radiating from the center and permeating our entire Being.

We learn from the first contact with Existence and Being that it was always there, waiting for us to move inward and find it. And in time, we learn that we can find it everywhere, as the upholder of all creation. It dwells just beyond the trees and rocks, the veiled mountains, beyond man. There is no place in space and no state of consciousness outside Existence and Being. It does not matter whether we can walk into a garden and sit in front of a small shrine, or we are bedridden. We offer our day wherever we are and enter our still center and experience the Presence which dwells in there and everywhere. A chapel effect aids our purpose but is of little importance. The setting is only a sop to the senses. What matters is that we make our offering before the distractions of the day begin.

When you enter our room to give us the morning washup and hair-combing and prepare us for breakfast, you distract us. No matter how many times during the day we may find the moment to practice the ritual, the early morning is the best—the time we rise from the silence of sleep with a more sensitive inward hearing. The unpleasant clamor of the world has not forced our attention outward. In the first hours of the day, our environment stirs into activity with the now-and-then sound of a car motor starting, or an occasional early delivery-truck driving by. Someone snores with a gentle rhythm. A bird warbles a note or two in the spreading light, but that is all.

These days our thoughts turn to the great mystery ahead. We watch for hints. We wonder, as a traveler wonders, about the country we are about to enter but have never seen before. We feel a thrill of expectancy like taking our first trip on a jet plane, except this trip is much more of an adventure than any plane trip or any flight of an astronaut into outer space. We will travel to another state of consciousness.

As with the astronauts, we have a launching pad, although ours is berthed to this physical life, where we have just finished our schooling. On the berth is a scaffolding that holds the capsule of our being—our still center. The capsule alone will launch from here. We see the whole design and feel the excitement, the anticipation that precedes the takeoff. We practice entering the capsule of our Being, shutting out the rest of the world.

Often, we imagine what the unknown is like. We wonder about those we have loved and who have made the trip before us. Some of us, while still in our cumbersome bodies, have caught a glimpse of the companions, or have felt their presence, in a draft of fresh air that had no natural source. We are sure that if only our sight were a little more penetrating, we could see them. As it is, we feel as though we are peering through sleep-heavy eyes.

How will we transition into their world? Must we first go to sleep? It would seem so.

We recall that the great poets, dramatists, and spiritual writers have called the passing between our present state of consciousness and the next *a sleep*. Familiar phrases come to mind:

A long, long sleep, a famous sleep, said Emily Dickinson.
He sleeps in Abraham's bosom, teaches the Old Testament.
Our little life is rounded with a sleep, said Shakespeare.

Rounded with *a sleep*? Yes. Just as each day is rounded by night. We like this idea. It gives our imagination a defined space to move about.

Of course, it is only a remembrance of one thing to another, but it holds together. The more we consider this likeness, the more confident we feel that the transition to the next life will be like falling asleep. At the end of every day, we transition from one state of consciousness to another. We think nothing of this change. At night, when we lie down on our beds, we are not bothered by the knowledge that soon we will lose all contact with the familiar objects around us, go to strange places, and take part in unusual experiences. Also, we will leave our bodies lying here on our beds and will assume an anomalous form. What we will take with us is our inner self, our Being. In the experience of sleep, you are always you—I am always I.

During our sleeping experience, we rarely remember anything about the bodies we leave behind, although sometimes we can see them lying on our beds as something quite apart from our life in the dream. But awareness of the "I" does not leave us. The "I" is like a chain strung with the beads of our ascending levels of consciousness. In our lives, we have been ill and have experienced discomfort. Some of us may experience illness as we are about to discard our bodies, but it has nothing to do with the transition itself, which is falling asleep. The gentle passage is greater when you do not use inhuman methods to keep us as long as you can in bodies we have already discarded. Do not turn our moment of dignity into one of degradation.

Disease can occur at any period of growth. If we experience it just before we leave, we welcome the change that will rescue us from what will seem like a bad dream when we wake up healed.

THE GRADUATES

We are at a gala night performance of a theater. The house lights go out, and the footlights come on, but the curtain has not yet risen. We sense the activity on the stage, the motion of the actors taking their places, the heightened aliveness of the moment. Everyone is waiting for the curtain to rise on a new drama. We hear familiar voices and see forms passing back and forth beyond our space.

What is this state of expectancy we are experiencing? For some of us, it may be the last phase of senility or a coma. Some of us experience this while the rational mind is in control—a doubtful blessing, for a sensible mind interferes with the wonder of the otherness that we experience. We do not need reason now. We only need awareness.

I mentioned senility. Did that word bother you—that fine, proud word which once referred to the Senate and seniority—that honored word? What we know about senility comes from observing a man or a woman, withdrawn and silent, or someone in a vague, childish regression, forever complaining about his physical discomfort and making a nuisance of himself. What you see is only the discarded body expressing itself, the senescence of the body.

The body is like the fallen leaf of a magnolia tree. The leaf drifts about the dry August air and makes a rustling sound as it scrapes over the terrace of ivy while the tree lifts its magnificent white blossoms high against the sky. The tree has nothing to do with the sound of the fallen leaf. Or the body is like the riverbed, parched and cracked, while the sweet water flows far beneath. The underground river has no connection to the dry surface where it once flowed.

The separation between Body and Being is all but complete in us. Being does not experience the senescence of the body but the height of enlightenment—the most blessed state we can know on earth, one steeped in love and confidence.

Anxiety had filled our active lives. But we have learned to trust the natural order of all things. The book of our lives is a complete experience. We read the ending and know how the story ends. The purpose of the beginning and the middle is clear to us. The main plot and subplots lead to the only conclusion: the book is a story of a school, a student, and the teacher. It is the story of progress in learning, of examinations passed and failed, and of the final promotion.

The story is also a romance between the student and the teacher, and, as in all love stories, the student, becomes enthralled with the teacher. Because of the student's state of captive ecstasy, the students in the lower grades call him "senile" or refer to him as someone in his second childhood.

As we reread the book of our school years, we see that no problem is too difficult for us to solve and that the difficulties solved are the steps by which we mount to a higher place. The law that makes this overwhelms us: our little lives, our small country, our little planet.

Man dares to travel into outer space because he is confident the same law will prevail wherever he goes, that he can pass from one level of consciousness to another, from dimension to dimension without wandering beyond that law which created us and will sustain us.

This knowledge creates confidence. All that we require is to pay attention to our intuition to see the wonders of the law that governs all things, and that we take part in furthering its purpose. We no longer feel anxiety, doubt, or fear.

In a tranquil half-sleep, we float on a sea of love protected as once we were in the womb. The turmoil of the world can no longer reach us, and the waters of forgetfulness have washed away all disturbing memories. We float in a prenatal dream, waiting for our new birth.

"Do not disturb" reads the warning supplied to sleeping guests. "Please, do not disturb," we would ask if we could. "The-about-to-be-born are sleeping." We need this gentle, healing sleep, this Lethean sleep of forgetfulness.

In a sheltered cave, the ancient-of-days slept himself into the Spirit World, according to a custom of an American Indian people. He was left alone to make a quiet transition in peace. We, too, plead that you allow us that peace as we drift on the brooding sea.

What infinite well-being is ours!

At times we are aware of the whispering voices of emissaries concerned with the comfort of our passage. The air we breathe is balmy. It stirs slightly, and there is the scent of flowers.

Nothing is an effort now.

Sometimes we see a glowing light that draws us into its very heart, and sometimes we see such beauty that our still-mortal eyes open wide with radiant joy.

www.ingramcontent.com/pod-product-compliance
Lightning Source LLC
Chambersburg PA
CBHW070952080526
44587CB00015B/2268